'FAMOUS BY MY SWORD'

The Army of Montrose and the Military Revolution

Charles Singleton

'This is the Century of the Soldier', Falvio Testir, Poet, 1641

Helion & Company

Helion & Company Limited
26 Willow Road
Solihull
West Midlands
B91 1UE
England
Tel. 0121 705 3393
Fax 0121 711 4075
Email: info@helion.co.uk
Website: www.helion.co.uk
Twitter: @helionbooks
Visit our blog http://blog.helion.co.uk/

Designed and typeset by Farr out Publications, Wokingham, Berkshire
Cover designed by Paul Hewitt, Battlefield Design (www.battlefield-design.co.uk)
Printed by Henry Ling Limited, Dorchester, Dorset

Cover: Montrose's Irish Brigade at the Battle of Aberdeen, 13 September 1644. (Painting by Peter Dennis, © Helion & Company Limited)

ISBN 978-1-909384-97-2

British Library Cataloguing-in-Publication Data.
A catalogue record for this book is available from the British Library.

For details of other military history titles published by Helion & Company Limited contact the above address, or visit our website: http://www.helion.co.uk.

We always welcome receiving book proposals from prospective authors.

Contents

Acknowledgements

I would like to thank Professor Malcolm Wanklyn and Martin Marix Evans for advice on writing and publishing. Thank you also to artist Peter Dennis for the front cover, George Anderson for the maps, and to my publisher Duncan Rogers. I would also like to acknowledge the expert advice of Stephen Brohan, Warwick Louth, Stephen Ede Borrett ,Glyn Hargreaves, Will Hughes, Gary Ashby, Alan Turton (for his 'salvo' line drawing), Hugh Logan (for his photograph and explanatory text and discussion on the Irish 'Montero') and the members of the Irish living history group, Claiomh. Very special thanks for my parents Trevor and Elizabeth. Thank you for the useful maxim given twenty years ago, "1644 good infantry, 1645 good cavalry".

Dedicated to my wife Helen, with much love.

Chronology of the First Civil War in Scotland and related events

1644

January 19	Scots under Leven invade England.
February 5	Cavalry fight at Corbridge in Northumberland between Scots under Lord Balgonie and English under Sir Marmaduke Langdale, who seems to have had the best of it.
March 7	Rearguard action at Penshaw Hill by Scots withdrawing into Sutherland.
March 16	Scots under Colonel William Stewart capture South Shields.
March 25	Indecisive battle at Boldon Hill near Sunderland between Leven's Scots and Newcastle's English Northern Royalist army.
April 13	Dumfries briefly occupied by Royalist rebels under Montrose.
April 18	Siege of York begins.
April 21	Town of Montrose stormed by rebels under Irvine of Drum and Nathaniel Gordon.
July 2	The battle of Marston Moor. The Scots under the generalship of Lord Leven made a substantial contribution to the allied victory over Rupert and Newcastle. Royalist control of Northern England is lost.
July 8	Irish troops land on west coast of Scotland.
July 16	York surrenders to allied army.
September 1	Rebels under Montrose defeat government forces at Tippermuir, outside Perth.
September 13	Rebels under Montrose defeat government forces at Aberdeen.
October 28	Indecisive battle at Fyvie Castle, between Montrose and a Covenant Army led by Argyll.

1645

February 2	Government forces defeated at Inverlochy by Montrose.
February 18	Regular cavalry regiment led by Lord Gordon defects to rebels, causing fall of Elgin.
March 15	Rebel quarters in Aberdeen beaten up by Sir John Hurry.
April 4	Rebels storm Dundee but then narrowly escape destruction by government forces under Hurry and William Baillie.
April 20	Doune Castle seized by rebels.

May 9	Montrose and his army are nearly surprised at Auldearn by Hurry, but fierce resistance by Irish and Gordon's regulars saves the day.
June 28	Carlisle surrenders to David Leslie.
July 2	Baillie defeated by Rebels at Alford.
July 30	Scots under Leven lay siege to Hereford.
August 15	Rebels attacked by Baillie at Kilsyth. Numbers of foot were approximately even but the rebels outnumbered Baillie's horse. The Government forces are totally routed.
September 5	Siege of Hereford lifted.
September 13	A much reduced army under Montrose is utterly defeated at Philiphaugh near Selkirk by David Leslie.
November 28	Scots under Leven lay siege to Newark on Trent.
1646	
April	Montrose besieges Inverness.
May 5	King Charles surrenders.
May 14	Aberdeen stormed by Huntly.
June 5	Battle of Benburb (Ulster), an Irish Confederate victory.
September 3	Ordered to cease hostilities, Montrose leaves Scotland for exile in Europe.

Introduction

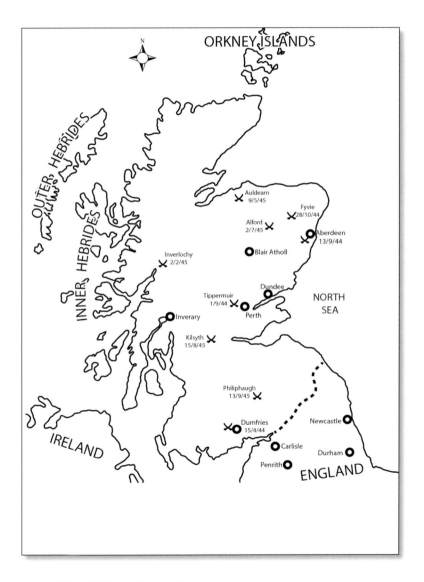

Scotland 1644-45. (George Anderson)

The start of the 17th Century for many historians sees the beginning of a revolution in military affairs. Many argue this is a period of rapid growth, of the reorganisation of armies, and the way these new forces and the state prosecuted war. The middle of the century was to see the first contact on a large scale between these new armies and the peoples of the Celtic Fringe.

The period is frequently perceived as a Gaelic 'Golden Age' of military success, where traditional Celtic martial methods sweep all before them, especially those opponents who seemingly appear well acquainted with the latest European innovations.

The most famous Celtic army of this era is the Royalist army of the Marquess of Montrose. Despite extensive revisionist work by writers such as Stuart Reid, there would still seem to be a mystical and mythical shroud that covers the whole subject of Celtic military competency during this period. Many writers still tend to concentrate and over-emphasise the role played by the Highland clansmen, and tend to ignore the ever-increasing numbers of regular troops that were present in every 'Highland Army'.

This intention of this book is to explore and analyse the nature and composition of the army of the Marquess of Montrose, and place it within a greater European context. It will argue that, despite its unique place in military history and folklore, this army, like the others in Western Europe of this period, also felt the influence of the changes and developments initiated by the European military revolution.

1

The Armies of the Early 17th Century

Scotland, like the rest of the British Isles, was to see minimal military activity in the early half of the 17th Century. However, Scots did not live in a vacuum. The news sheets telling of the wars in Europe and plethora of books giving advice on soldierly conduct meant that those of a soldierly persuasion were easily able to follow the current trends in military innovation.

When the need to arm came in the late 1630s as a response to Charles I's attempts at religious reform, military development was to follow very similar lines to advancements elsewhere in Central and Western Europe. Many officers and men would return home bringing with them their experience of fighting in the new European ways, and along with them would come prestigious amounts of modern military hardware. The years from 1639 to 1644 were to see the import of weapons and equipment from the Continent on a significant scale. The Scottish agent in Zeeland was able to secure and send to Scotland 31,673 muskets, 29,000 swords, 8,000 pikes, 500 pairs of pistols and some 12 artillery pieces.

The Infantry

The standard infantry formation of the 1640s was the regiment. The ideal composition of a regiment was ten companies; one company each for the colonel, lieutenant colonel, major and the seven captains.

These companies between them, according to the military manuals of the time, should have had a combined strength of somewhere in the region of 1,200 men. The reality was radically different, with a regiment of 450-500 men considered a strong formation, and an optimum for command and control.

The infantry regiments fighting in England during this period aimed, as a general principal, for two muskets to every pike. This, however, was an ideal that was not achieved all the time and both Parliament and Crown frequently went into action with far lower ratios. However, as procurement procedures, production methods and supplies of firearms improved, it was not unheard of to have infantry regiments boasting ratios of one pike to three or even

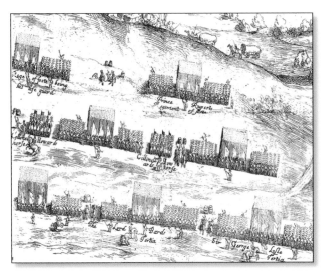

A close up of the map of Naseby from Joshua Sprigge's *Anglia Rediviva*, showing, in part, the deployment of the King's army at Naseby. It shows the mutually-supporting chequerboard deployment of infantry regiments and in particular the sleeves of musketeers supported by a central body of pike.

four muskets. The King's Oxford Army was to increasingly experiment with brigaded musket battalions during the second half of the First Civil War. George Lisle was to lead such formations as these at actions such as Cheriton and the Second Battle of Newbury. Similar experiments happened in Scotland. Whilst fighting against Montrose, a Major Haldane was leading a battalion of musketeers as an advanced guard at Kilsyth in 1645.

Regiments in the Army of the Covenant, the national army of Scotland, it would seem, fielded greater numbers of pike, often in the ratio of three muskets to every two pikes. Traditionally, this has mistakenly been identified as due either to poor economic conditions making the supply of firearms prohibitive, or a general backwardness in military affairs. A more reasoned argument would be to suggest that with so many Scottish troops and officers having served in the Swedish Army, they would adopt a similar practice. Tactical doctrine within the Swedish army called for an aggressive infantry arm, with musketeers 'shooting onto target', the pikemen would exploit the disorder caused from the firearm casualties. Furthermore, the traditional notion that the pike was a defensive arm to defend the musketeer whilst loading and against cavalry attack can also be discounted. Practise had shown that cavalry attack could, at times, be foolhardy against massed bodies of infantry. Indeed at Marston Moor, when Royalist cavalry brigade commander Sir Charles Lucas had led his victorious cavalry, without supporting infantry, into the flank of the exposed Scottish infantry he was captured and his troops driven off. Irish musketeers were able to practically destroy a cavalry unit (albeit a small one) that charged into them during the Battle of Aberdeen.

The Cavalry

Despite the growing ascendancy of the infantry soldier, thanks largely to firepower, the horse was seen by most as the battle-winning weapon. Whilst the infantry sought to out-manoeuvre and pin the enemy's battle line, it would be the cavalry that dealt the telling blow.

During the 1640s, three distinct types of horseman were to be seen in the British Isles. The lancer, although listed in returns for the English trained bands of the 1620s and 1630s, had ceased to be used in England. The cuirassier, whilst still heavily employed on the Continent (albeit evolving into a lighter horseman, by the 1640s), was not a common sight in the British Isles. The cost of both equipment and a horse big and strong enough to carry an armoured trooper made the large-scale deployment of cuirassier units prohibitive. Some units were raised, however - a troop of gentleman volunteers fought for the Scottish Royalist cause at Megray Hill in 1639, and Sir Arthur Heselrige fielded his famous regiment of 'Lobsters'.

These units were on the whole shortlived and by 1644 the dominant form of cavalry in the British Isles was the 'harquebusier'. Originally classed as a light horseman, the harquebusier was to become the universal horse soldier. The cavalry writer, John Vernon, was to describe them as being equipped thus:

> … his defensive arms, are only an open Caske or Head-peece, a back and breast plate with a buff coate … his offensive armes are a good Harquebus or Carbine … and two good firelock pistols in houlsters. At his saddle a good stiffe sword … and a good poll-axe in his hand, a good tall horse of fifteen handfuls high, strong and nimble'

The harquebusier was to be the standard form of cavalry within the Scots Government armies, and in much smaller numbers amongst the Scottish Royalist forces too. The defection to Montrose of a regiment of regular horse in early 1645 was to give the King's general a much-needed strike force. The timely counter-attacks of such cavalry under the leadership of Lords Aboyne and Gordon at Auldearn reversed a defeat into victory for Montrose.

A regiment of horse was, in theory, to consist of 500 men and officers, divided in six to eight troops, as was the case with the infantry regimental establishments, and organisation would vary dramatically.

The Scottish cavalry arm was much weaker than its English counterpart. This was due to the lack of quality mounts and little or no tradition in horse breeding within Scotland. Although many Scots troopers were equipped in a similar fashion to their English counterparts, attempts were made to compensate for the lack of numbers and quality of horseflesh.

Possibly in order to bring some effectiveness to the Scottish cavalry arm and improve performance there was a heavy reliance by some units on carrying as many firearms as was possible. In 1638, a Scottish trooper was described as equipped with ' … five shot, with a carbine in his hand, two pistols by his side and another two by his saddle'.

Further firepower could be added to the cavalry by the addition of troops of dragoons onto the regiment's establishments. The dragoon, a relative new form of soldier, was essentially a musketeer on horseback. The dragoon's role was to act as scout and lend extra fire support on the battlefield where needed. Captain John Mortimer led a small troop of dragoons in Montrose's army. Formed from O'Cahan's infantry regiment, it was essentially a mobile force for raiding.

The Scots were to make extensive use of the lance, and many contemporaries wrote of their efficiency with them. Irish horse refused to fight against Scottish lance-armed troopers unless issued with armour, and Scots lancers led by David Leslie were to make a telling intervention against the flank of the Royalist cavalry at Marston Moor. Even the vaunted Ironsides, the elite cavalry of the New Model, were brought to check by lance-armed Scots. In the confused fighting following the Battle of Preston in 1648, the pursuing New Model troopers were worsted, and Colonel Francis Thornhaugh was mortally wounded.

The Ordnance

An essential part of the modern mid-17th Century army was the artillery train, described by Clarendon as 'a sponge that can never be filled or satisfied'.

Scottish government forces had a traditionally strong well-developed artillery arm dating back to the 16th Century. Lord Leven was to take the Army of the Solemn League and Covenant into England in early 1644 with an extensive artillery train. An estimated 69 major pieces of ordnance and 88 lesser pieces accompanied the army. The contribution to the number of artillery pieces fielded by the combined allied armies at Marston Moor by the Scots boosted numbers to 100 guns on the field, with roughly 1 gun to 300 men. Fighting in Prussia in 1806, Napoleon was able to field one gun for every 600 men

Artillery was to feature in the armies fielded against Montrose, but was to have minimal impact. The mobile nature of the campaign fought by both sides in the north-east of Scotland in 1644-45 made extensive use prohibitive. The notable exception to this was arguably the deployment of artillery by the Government forces at Aberdeen. Guns, deployed ahead of the Government army's centre was to sting the Royalist centre into the advance, and quickly overrun them.

The Scots abroad

Alexander Leslie had a long and successful career as a soldier; attaining the rank of a Dutch captain, a Swedish field marshal and, in Scotland, the title Earl of Leven. From 1605-7, he served under Sir Horace Vere, one of the great English captains fighting in the Netherlands. Entering Swedish service in 1608, Leslie was knighted by King Gustavus Adolphus in 1626. His period of service with the Swedes would have seen the development and introduction of many of the Swedish King's famous military reforms and innovations. In 1638 he returned to Scotland following the emerging crisis surrounding the signing of the Covenant, bringing with him much-needed equipment, military experts and years of experience in the modern European ways of war.

Alexander Leslie, 1st Earl of Leven, c 1580-1661.

David Leslie joined the Swedish army as a captain to Alexander Leslie. By 1634, he was colonel of a cavalry regiment and fought in some of the major battles of the Thirty Years War. Although he returned in 1640 to join the Army of the Covenant, Leslie did not take part in the fighting during the Bishops' Wars. When the Scots invaded England again in January 1644, Leslie was appointed Lieutenant-General to Alexander Leslie, the Earl of Leven. Leading a brigade of horse supporting Cromwell's cavalry, his timely flank attack (although never recognised by Cromwell) helped drive Rupert's troopers from the field at the Battle of Marston Moor in July 1644.

In September 1645, he was recalled to Scotland to deal with Montrose. Leading a veteran cavalry brigade, he made short work of the Marquess at Philiphaugh. Although Montrose was able to escape and rebuild his army, his defeat at the hands of Leslie was to herald the end of his year of victories. Returning to England, he supervised the siege and surrender of Newark and, indeed, of the King in May 1646. Taking no part in the Engager invasion of 1648, he was to be appointed the commander in chief of the Covenanter army in 1650. Although he was to skilfully out-manoeuvre Cromwell following the English invasion the same year, he threw away the

David Leslie, 1600-1682.

gained advantage and was decisively beaten, firstly at Dunbar and then a year later at Worcester in September 1651. King Charles II raised him to the peerage as 1st Baron Newark in 1661 in recognition of his services to the Royalist cause.

2

The Scots and the 'Military Revolution'

Historians of the early modern period have, over the past forty years or more, attempted to define the nature and chronological location of a 'Military Revolution'. Because of the length of wars, improvements in fortification designs and advances in firearm technology, armies became more permanent and increasingly larger, with better discipline. The resulting financial costs obliged rulers to control their resources more effectively through the reform, centralisation and improvement of their administration, fiscal apparatus and the reduction of local interests and franchises. This resulted in most governments, whether monarchical or republican, becoming both increasingly centralised and absolute.[1] The Military Revolution debate evolved after the publication in 1967 of Michael Roberts' *Essays in Swedish History*. Roberts, whilst following the main trend of changes in military affairs from 1580 to the middle of the 17th Century, sees the true champions of the revolution as the Netherlands of William of Orange, and the Sweden of Gustavus Adolphus. He argues that the development of these armies required large central administrations and funding by the state, which was to lead ultimately to the era of absolutism in Western Europe. Roberts' theory was popular, as it followed contemporary thinking and remained unchallenged until Geoffrey Parker's modifications in his 1988 book *The Military Revolution*. Whilst acknowledging previous ideas, Parker argues the case that the Spanish army of the period was a true innovator, being more receptive to new ideas and more flexible than it had previously been given credit for. Parker broadens the scope of the debate by arguing that major changes occurred in artillery, siege warfare and the mass manufacture of cheap gunpowder infantry weapons. He also goes on to consider the impact of seapower and the effect these innovations in Europe had on the wider world.

One of the most significant contributions to the debate was made in Jeremy Black's 1991 publication, *A Military Revolution? Military Change and European Society, 1550-1800*. Black moves away from the traditional arguments and sees the developments of the late 17th Century as the most

1. Childs, John, *Warfare in the 17th Century*, (London 2001), p.16.

important. He argues against the perception of Sweden as the 'market leaders' of the period. Indeed, he claims that Swedish success at Breitenfeld (17 September 1631) was not due to tactical innovations. He argues further that other Western European powers employed similar tactical methodology, and the universal practice of hiring mercenaries and former prisoners of war led to the mutual cross-fertilisation of ideas. The main factor, Black feels, was the size of armies; Breitenfeld had seen 42,000 well-equipped, well-fed and motivated Swedes and their allies defeat less than 35,000 half-starved, poorly-equipped and motivated Imperialists. Yet, on more equal terms, a supposedly obsolescent Imperial army was able to inflict a bloody and crippling draw at Lützen (6 November 1632), which saw the cream of the Swedish army, along with their King, perish on the field. Both the Swedes and the French, inheritors of the Swedish tradition, were to suffer repeated reversals of this nature until the end of the war in 1648.

The principal developments of the military revolution took place in the heartland of Western Europe, war-torn Germany and the besieged Netherlands. It was here that the new theories were put into practice and the lessons sometimes, but not always, learned. Countries around the epicentre of the revolution embraced the new ideas and developments, whilst those further afield, such as Poland fighting the Muscovite, Turk and Tartar, adapted the new ideas to their particular circumstances. Even the wilds of the Celtic Fringe, the outer limits of Western Europe, were affected; the Earl of Tyrone's Irish rebel troops as early as the 1590s were considered better shots with firearms than their English counterparts.[2]

The contribution to military developments made during this time-frame by the Scots is frequently overlooked. During the period in question, one of Scotland's principal exports was men, in the form of mercenaries, to fight in the European wars. In Scotland's harsh economic environment, the lure of money, adventure and booty drew many to the colours. From 1620 to 1637, large numbers of the Scots male population were to serve in the armies of the Netherlands, France, Denmark and Russia. Royal Warrants in 1624, 1626-29, 1631-33 and 1637, were to permit the recruitment of 41,400 Scots for European armies. Some 20-30,000 Scots saw service in the Swedish army alone (approximately 2-3% of a pre-civil war population of 1,000,000).[3] Indeed, so successful were the efforts of the recruiting agents (the most famous, Donald Mackay recruited over 10,000 men for the continent) that by 1628 the country had been emptied of potential recruits to such an extent that restrictions keeping recruitment to the Highlands and islands were put in place.[4] Many Scots were to achieve fame and high rank overseas; none

2. One observer was to view Irish as 'as good marksmen as France, Flanders or Spain can show'. Firearms and gunpowder production were started by the Irish rebels as early as the1580s. Heath, Ian, *The Irish Wars 1485-1603* (Oxford 1993), pp.13-14.

3. Based on figures from Carlton, Charles, *Going to the Wars - The Experience of the British Civil Wars, 1638-1651*, (London 1992), p.214. The figures suggested for population losses should be treated with caution. See also Furgol, Edward M., 'Scotland Turned Sweden: The Scottish Covenanters and the Military Revolution, 1638-1651', in John Morrill (ed.), *The Scottish National Covenant in its British Context 1638-1651*, (Edinburgh, 1990), p.136.

4. Donald Mackay's recruiting was to be immortalised in the Gaelic proverb 'He who is down on luck, can still get a dollar from Mackay'. Brzezinski, Richard, 'British Mercenaries in the Baltic, 1560-1683 (2)' in *Military Illustrated*, no 6, April/May, 1987, p.29.

James Graham, Marquess of Montrose, 1612-1650. Portrait attributed to van Honthorst.

more so than the Earl of Leven, Alexander Leslie, who entered Swedish service in 1605. In 1636 he was promoted to Field Marshal.

It was men such as Leven who returned to his country in the troubled times of the late 1630s, taking weapons and munitions in lieu of back pay. In response to Charles I's attempted religious and political reforms, the National Covenant was created. This act of self-defence and open defiance was not that of a small reactionary movement, but of the government and state. The determination to defend their ideals, which would soon be coupled with the need to protect co-religionists from atrocities committed when violent rebellion erupted in Ireland, led to the need for an army. Unlike England that had a countrywide system of militia, known as the Trained Bands, Scotland's organic defence forces, known as Fencibles, were restricted to the urban 'Royal Burghs'. Thus, any military force that was raised was done so from scratch. It can be argued with some measure that this army, unlike most of the European armies of the period which relied heavily on foreign mercenaries, was almost entirely home-grown and thus possibly one of, if not *the* first, truly national armies of the modern era.

The huge numbers of veteran soldiers, like Leven, now returning home, endowed the creation of the army with a large professional core on which to build. Based on Swedish administrative and recruiting models, this army was able to dictate peace to Charles in the Bishops' Wars, defeat pro-royalist factions, and intervene in the Irish rebellion. Rapid expansion followed in 1643 after the signing of the 'Solemn League and Covenant', which allied the Scottish nation with the English Parliament. The Army of the Covenant invaded England and made a major contribution to the outcome of the war. Between 1639 and 1651, the Scottish nation maintained an army which was able to operate from the Orkneys in the north, to Hereford in the south and fight a war on three fronts (England, Ireland and against Montrose and Huntley in the north east of Scotland). Thanks to the infrastructure of the state, which supported it, the army was able, after numerous defeats and reverses, to recover and remain in the field. However, despite the forward-looking nature of the national army, it is its opponents that seem to command most attention, particularly the Scots pro-Royalist army led by James Graham, Marquess of Montrose.

Montrose's own life and adventures are shrouded in a veneer of romance and myth. Originally a supporter of the Covenant, he became alienated from the movement and in the summer of 1644, was to be found in the Scottish Highlands leading a mixed Scots-Irish Royalist army against government forces. His military reputation soon passed into legend. He was seen to have a leadership style and charisma which rallied men to him. Thus, his troops, without pay and in poor conditions, were able to inflict a series of spectacular defeats on the Covenant troops sent against them. Martyrdom was to add to the legend when he was finally defeated, betrayed, and executed in Edinburgh on 21 May 1651.

The men he fought with are also seen in the same mythical proportions, being described at the one extreme by Geoffrey Parker as 'undisciplined clansmen armed with traditional weapons' (much to the chagrin of Edward Furgol)[5], or at the other, as for the main part 'brought up in West Flanders, expert soldiouris, with ane yeiris pay'.[6] The above contradiction, coupled with contemporary writers' sometimes sycophantic preoccupation with Montrose, rather than the more useful, but perhaps less glamorous account of every day life in the army, has led to a great deal of misunderstanding about it. The matter is further complicated by many people's perception of Scottish Highland life, culture and military prowess, influenced in part by Robert Burns and Sir Walter Scott and, more recently, by the film *Braveheart*.[7] Even today, many people see the Highlands as Scotland, and all Scotsmen as Highlanders. It is even possible to argue that with the growth of the Scottish nationalist movement, many print houses and authors have, as with the Jacobite rebellions, set their own political agendas on the subject, thus placing yet another slant on the topic.

---

5. Furgol, Edward M, 'Scotland Turned Sweden: The Scottish Covenanters and the Military Revolution, 1638-1651', in John Morrill (ed.), *The Scottish National Covenant in its British Context 1638-1651*, (Edinburgh, 1990), p.148.
6. Spalding, John, *Memorialls of the Trubles in Scotland 1627-1645* (Aberdeen, 1850), p.385.
7. Davidson, Neil, *The Origins of Scottish Nationhood* (London, 2000), pp.129-132.

3

Overall View of the Army

Whereas the civil war in England was a conflict between two quasi-legitimate governments, each holding sway over specific geographical territories and both being able to keep forces in the field, this was not to be the case in Scotland. Here, the Royalists were rebelling against what had essentially been, since 1638, an independent republican government. With no equivalent of the Oxford Parliament or headquarters in the country, and as a result no formal form of government, the Royalist rebels had no access to regular troops. Being unable, as they were, to hold onto any sizeable amounts of territory for any length of time, the Royalists could not make use of the militia system for the raising and fielding of troops in any serious numbers.[1] These factors resulted in the army having an ever-changing nature, and for all intents and purposes to be very much a partisan movement.

Despite the ever-changing outward appearance of the army, there are a number of features that remain constant throughout its history. The popular image of Montrose leading an all-conquering Highland host, armed with the ancient weapons of the Gael – broadsword, claymore and targe – can now be convincingly laid aside. The army can be seen as comprising two distinct parts: Highland clans and a large core of conventionally armed professional Irish mercenaries and lowland Scots, one part of the army regular, the other irregular. The use of irregular auxiliaries was not uncommon in European warfare. Both the Holy Roman Empire and the Turks used large numbers of irregular troops in their never-ending border warfare. The French, for almost a century beforehand, were making extensive use of Albanian light horse, known as Stradiots. This practice was widely used in the British Isles since Anglo-Norman times. The Scottish Royal army was traditionally able to call upon contingents from the Highlands and Islands whilst, in the period under discussion, one of the leading lights of the Covenant, the Marquess of Argyll, was able to call upon a private army composed of men from his own clan, the Campbells. This force he used partly as paramilitary police force and partly as the tool of strong-arm tactics.[2] Both England and Scotland, during the conflicts of the 15th, 16th and 17th centuries, were to make

---

1. Barratt, John, *Cavaliers: The Royalist Army at War 1642-46* (Stroud, 2000), p.145.
2. Stevenson, David, *Highland Warrior: Alasdair MacColla and the Civil Wars,* (Edinburgh, 1980), pp.19, 45.

much use of the Border Reivers, an indigenous form of the irregular light horseman. Although in terminal decline in the British Isles by the period under discussion, this form of auxiliary was a still very popular, if not even an essential part, of many European armies.[3] Conversely, the 'irregular' was to see the benefit of the regular too. Clan chieftains of the Western Highlands were to make great use in 1588 of marooned survivors of the Spanish Armada in settling scores with their rivals.

Although still relatively new in the British Isles, the regular, professional soldier had been a common feature of European armies for a considerable length of time. However, the introduction and rapid ascendancy of black powder weapons was to bring along with them many changes. Whereas the soldier of the Middle Ages had essentially been an individualist, trained over a long period of time, the firearm was to demand new skills. Now the soldier was required to act in unison with a considerable number of others. Arquebus and musket drill could contain upwards of ninety-six movements, all to be carried out in a synchronised manner which, coupled with counter marching, was aimed to provide a safe (large bodies of troops, considerable quantities of black powder and each soldier carrying a length of lit match cord, do not a good mix make) continuous rate of fire.[4] The expense of these new weapons led to large numbers of troops being maintained throughout the year on a permanent basis for the first time in modern history, rather than disbandment at the end of each campaigning season.

These new developments had largely bypassed the British Isles which had, for the main, enjoyed peace since the start of the century. It was only in the troubled period prior to the start of the Civil Wars, that professionally led and maintained troops started to appear in the British Isles. As discussed previously in the text, when the Scottish nation saw the need to defend itself, it was to make full use of the latest European developments brought back by its returning veterans.

The Scottish Royalists, on the whole, were unable to control and manage any significant amounts of territory from which to raise funding and conscripts. However, the methods used by them to support their forces were very similar to regional armies in the rest of the British Isles. Like the provincial armies of the warring factions in England, Montrose had hoped for support from the Royalist central government in Oxford. Like the Royalist satellite armies, he was to be on the whole frequently disappointed. Despite initial promises of support, it was to be only after news of his early victories reached the outside world that the Irish Confederacy, through negotiations with the King, agreed to support him.[5] This support was, however, to be very limited. The Royalist central government also attempted to support Montrose directly. Under the direction of a certain Captain Allen, one of the Queen's purchasing agents, £10,000 worth of arms and ammunition was sent to Montrose from France and Holland, some of which was, however, to fall into enemy hands.[6]

---

3. Durham, Keith, *The Border Reivers* (London, 1995), p.33.
4. Roberts, Michael, 'The Military Revolution 1560-1660', in Clifford J. Rogers, (ed.), *The Military Revolution Debate* (Oxford, 1995), p.14.
5. Edwards, Peter, *Dealing in Death, The Arms Trade and the British Civil Wars, 1638-52* (Stroud, 2000), p.187.
6. Williams, Ronald, *Montrose, Cavalier in Mourning*, (London, 1975), p.300.

Although Irish and 16th, not 17th Century, this image of Kern raiding a settlement would have been typical of the Scots Highlanders' normal run of activities. Taken from Derrick's *The Image of Ireland* (1581).

Diplomatic efforts were made by the King to secure support for Montrose. The Danish were offered the Shetlands and Orkneys, in return for cavalry, arms and cash. These negotiations, however, came to nothing. Substantial support did, however, develop and a considerable amount of match, shot, powder, cannons and other equipment were organised for delivery from the continent. This shipment left the Baltic in early July 1646 but by then it was too late, for Montrose disbanded his forces on 22 July.[7]

Finding themselves not being able to gather central funding and support, Montrose's army was soon to develop procurement methods and techniques that were to resemble closely those used by other provincial forces. The most common method of fundraising used was that of the *Brandschatzung* or 'fire raid'. Here, a community would be approached by a body of troops, who would threaten to destroy property and livestock unless a given amount of cash and commodities was handed over.[8] Although Prince Rupert is frequently accused of introducing the practice into the country, it is probable that it was also brought to the British Isles by those Irish veterans who had served on the Continent and were also very familiar with the fire raid. A strong native tradition of the fire raid had been established along the Anglo-Scots border for centuries. Used by the Reivers, in a never-ending cycle

7. Edwards, p.187.
8. Roy, Ian, 'England turned Germany? The Aftermath of The Civil War in its European Context', *Transactions of the Royal Historical Society*, 5th Series, Vol.28, p.136.

of raiding and in fighting that until early 17th century, this form of gang warfare dominated the border Marches and 'debatable lands'. The nature of the Thirty Years War in Flanders, where the many of the Irish veterans had served, certainly encouraged this form of warfare. In this sector of the conflict, major engagements were on the whole rare, sieges and skirmishes being more common. It was common practice for the opposing forces frequently to 'beat up' each other's quarters in hit and run raids. In Europe at this time the civilian and his property, as much as the soldier, were to be considered legitimate targets. However, this form of raiding and extortion had been part of standard practice in the Scottish Isles for a considerable length of time, and more recently so in Ireland. On his entry into the city of Perth after the Battle of Tippermuir in 1644, Montrose requested that the corporation provide him with £1,300 worth of cloth in addition to cash and ammunition.[9] Aberdeen and Dundee were, however, not to be as fortunate and both were to suffer terribly at the hands of the Royalist armies, in sacks that were not dissimilar to those at Bolton, Leicester and Basing House or numerous other towns, villages and country houses.

---

9.   White, Iain, *Agriculture and Society in 17th Century Scotland,* (Edinburgh, 1979), p.17.

4

Highland Troops

MACLACHLAN.

The traditional Victorian stereotypical image of the Highland warrior. The reality was frequently very different. The seventeenth century was to see increasing numbers of the Highland Gael armed with modern European military hardware.

The traditional depiction of the Scots Royalist army is that of a clan army. This is hardly surprising, as not only does the Highlander have an overly romanticised image, but the popular perception of Montrose's army and the military prowess of the clansman are based on inaccurate, dated assumptions.

One of the greatest misconceptions of Highland society is the notion of it being a 'warrior society'. As with all supposed 'warrior societies', be it Afghan Hill Tribe, Biblical Sea Peoples or Scottish Highlander, only a small percentage of the population were of the warrior cast with any form of martial training. The bulk of the clan unit was formed by men lacking any form of discipline, training or suitable equipment. Thus, as can be seen, the vast majority of members of the clan did not conform to the traditional stereotype of a bloodthirsty warrior. The reality was that the great majority of the clan unit were peasants who had been, at best, dragged along by their landlords to make up the numbers. The distinction between the gentlemen who made up the warrior caste of the clan and the peasant at the other end of the spectrum can be emphasised by a survey of those Highlanders taken prisoner after the Battle of Culloden in 1746. Of the 565 prisoners below officer rank whose ages were recorded, over half were aged over thirty; ninety-one of them were over fifty, and a third were sixty or over.[1] Writing at roughly the same time, the English General Hawley was to describe the appearance of the typical Highland clan unit:

'They commonly form their front rank of what they call their best men, or True Highlanders, the number of which being always but few, when they

1. Seton, B.G & J.G. Arnot, *Prisoners of the '45* (Edinburgh, 1928), p.270.

In solchem Habit Gehen die 800 In Stettin angekommen Irrlander oder Irren.

The famous 'Stettin' Print, which depicts Highlanders (but calls them Irish) in Swedish service in 1631. The print is worthy of greater examination as it is one of the few illustrations of the period depicting Highland warriors dressed in contemporary Highland dress. It is also one of the earliest illustrations showing the easily recognizable Highland dress of kilts and tartan.

The heading above the print reads in English 'The 800 Irish that have arrived in Stettin are marching in this dress'. It's possible that the Scots' use of the Gaelic language led many Germans to believe they were Irish. The language barrier, coupled with their different appearance to Lowland Scots who were also fighting in Germany, would have no doubt added to the confusion.

Note how only one of them has a musket, and only two have swords of some description. None have shields. The bow was still popular in the Highlands. In the 1638 Atholl census some 130 men were noted as carrying bows along with other weapons. The musketeer is depicted holding his musket in the 'shouldered musket' posture, evidence of formal training in modern military practice.

form in battalions they commonly form four deep, and these Highlanders form the front of the four, the rest being Lowlanders and arrant scum.'[2]

Further evidence for the lack of martial orientation amongst the Highland Gael comes from the 1638 Atholl census. Of the 451 Highlanders recorded, only eleven lacked swords. Despite 100 possessing muskets, only 124, a quarter of those with swords, had targes (shields). Thus, roughly only a quarter were armed in what is seen as the traditional Gael manner, with sword, targe and musket.[3] These figures can be reinforced by further supporting evidence. A group of thirty men from the Island of Colonsay were described as being armed with fourteen muskets (with enough powder and shot for about twenty rounds each), twenty-four swords and seventeen shields.[4] Again, as with the Atholl statistics, the Colonsay figures would suggest that roughly a third of those Highlanders described seemingly fitted the archetypal portrayal of the traditional Gael warrior. The fact that Atholl was considered to be one of the more prosperous Highland regions with good access to Lowland markets, and Colonsay on the West coast of Scotland, a very much poorer and backward area, should have relatively similar statistical profiles argues convincingly against the notion of a warrior race with a strong martial tradition.[5]

A lack of traditional weaponry led to many clan retinues and 'regiments' becoming increasingly equipped with more readily available and contemporary equipment. During the First Bishops' War, a considerable amount of equipment was shipped by the King to his supporters in Scotland. This cargo was to include '2000 muscaties, bandilieris, and Muscat staves, 1000 pikis with harness and armour, both for foot men and horss men,

2. Tomasson, C. & F. Buist, *Battles of the '45* (London 1962), pp.93-94

3. Reid, Stuart, *Scots Armies of the 17th Century: The Royalist Armies 1639-46* (Leigh on Sea, 1989), pp.47-48 and 50-53.

4. Stephenson, p.43.

5. Macinnes, Allan, *Clanship, Commerce and the House of Stuart 1603-1788* (East Linton, 1996), pp.56-81.

The background of the 'Stettin' print in greater detail. . Although it has been argued that most Scots arriving in Germany were equipped and clothed in a conventional Western European style, there are references to 'red-shanks' and bare-legged Highlanders in Germany.

Similar to the musketeer in the foreground, these musketeers are posed in the 'shouldered musket' posture. Furthermore, the depiction of these Highlanders in rank and file would indicate that not only have they been trained in individual musket drill, but also, in addition, massed infantry formation and movement drill.

The flag depicting three crowns indicates that this is a Swedish formation, no doubt trained in the use of the 'Swedish Brigade' deployment, a notoriously complex system which required a high degree of discipline and training. It would be in such environment that those Highlanders that fought in the European wars would have learnt the latest military developments.

cairabins, horss peces, pistollis, pulder, leid and matche'.[6]

Regular troops were not the only ones to benefit from this delivery. Contemporary accounts from the period tell of various Highland chiefs, such as Donald Farquharson, equipping his and various other clan retinues with these weapons.[7] This process was to evolve throughout the Civil Wars. The Earl of Seaforth's regiment, formed from the men of his clan, albeit a Government unit, was equipped with muskets and pike in 1645.[8] The Tutor of Macleod's Clan Regiment, having run out of ammunition at the Battle of Worcester in 1651, fought on with clubbed muskets.[9]

Exposure to modern developments can be traced back even further. In 1615, to celebrate the creation of an alliance, Sir James MacDonald and his entourage were greeted by a drill display made by the followers of Coll Ciotach (Alastair MacColla's father), which was to involve marching and musket drill.[10] Not only would this suggest some form of military training, but a support structure and procurement process which was able to provide such equipment as shot, match and powder, not only in combat, but in training as well.

Despite extensive evidence that would argue for the lack of traditional Celtic martial expertise amongst the Highland clans, various theories have been put forward to explain their military successes. In the forefront of these ideas, is that of the 'Highland Charge'. The basic tenet of the charge was for the clan 'unit' to fire a volley with musket and then 'fall on' with sword and targe to exploit any confusion and disorder created by the volley.

6. Spalding, p.144.
7. Ibid., p.163.
8. Furgol, Edward, *A Regimental History of the Covenanting Armies 1639-1651*, (Edinburgh, 1990), p.237.
9. Atkin, Malcolm, *Cromwell's Crowning Mercy* (Stroud, 1998), p.89.
10. Stevenson, p.45.

The creation of the charge is frequently attributed to Alastair MacColla, who first used it at the Battle of Bendooragh, Ireland in 1641. A detailed account of the battle describes MacColla as directing his troops in the following manner:

> '… having commanded his murderers to lay downe all their fyre-arms … fell in amongst them (with swords and durcks) in such a furious and irresistible manner that it was reported that not a man of them escaped of all eight hundred.[11]

Stephenson and Hill both identify the introduction of the musket to the Celtic world and the adoption of the targe and single-handed sword as pre-requisites to the success of the charge.[12] Stevenson argues that these new weapons were essential to the development of the 'Highland Charge'. The earlier Irish practice of showering the enemy with darts, javelins and arrows, although effective, was now replaced by the use of the musket. The Highlanders might have used their muskets only once before abandoning them, but this volley was to be central to their tactics. Not only did this volley cause disorder among their opponents, but it would also lead, hopefully, to the reply in kind by the enemy, instead of them waiting until the Highlanders were at point blank range. Thus the Highlander could make a charge to contact in relative safety, while the enemy musketeers were attempting to reload. Hill goes as far to suggest that the Highland volley was, in addition, employed to create a smokescreen from which the charge could be staged.[13] Stevenson concludes by arguing that abandoning their most modern weapon in favour of one which was centuries old was a decision that, in light of the limitations of the musket, brought them great advantages at a critical moment on the battlefield.[14]

It is possible to challenge this view. The 1638 Atholl census would seem to indicate that with less than a quarter of the men present armed with muskets, and a similar number armed with sword and shield, the local clansmen lacked sufficient equipment to execute a 'Highland Charge' in the fashion described by Stevenson or Hill. The musket was a massed infantry weapon, only effective when used in very large numbers. The effects of a small number of muskets on the outcome of a firefight, when frequently less than 10% of ballistics found their mark, must have been negligible. Consideration must be taken of using firearms whilst under battle conditions. Competency with a firearm maybe one thing, but quite another whilst involved in a firefight.

This image is taken from a propaganda broadsheet of 1631, and is contemporaneous with the previous pictures. This depiction once again shows Highland troops in Germany. Again they are depicted marching in formation, whilst using the latest drill postures. The flags depicted are those of Sweden and Saxony, and represents their alliance.

11. Ibid., p.82.
12. Hill, James Michael, *Celtic Warfare 1595-1763* (Edinburgh, 1986), pp.47-48. See also Stevenson, p.83.
13. Hill, p.48. See also his article 'Killiecrankie and the Evolution of Highland Warfare' in *War in History*, Vol.1, 1994, pp.125-139.
14. Stevenson, p.83. For a further critical review of the Highland Charge see Reid, Stuart, *Highland Clansman 1689-1746* (Oxford, 1997).

A further surviving picture is from a German news sheet, again from 1631. It depicts 'Der Irlander' (an Irishman - but most probably a Highlander), 'der Lappe' (a Laplander), and 'der Finlander' (a Finn).

An examination of the 'Scot' shows he is wearing a sleeveless tartan long coat, and not a traditional plaid. He, along with the 'Lapp', is double-armed with bow and the more modern musket.

Whilst there are plenty of descriptions of the Highlander and his way of war (Hawley, Wade, Wishart et al.), there was seemingly no warning of the musketry volley preceding the charge.

Advocates of this argument fail to take into account the nature of 17th Century fire control. Regular soldiers who, by the 1640s fought in four to six rank deep formations, did not fire all their muskets at once, but rather in a continuous cycle of successive ranks. Thus, as the highlander charged home, he would still be under continuous musket fire.

The chief supporters of the Highland Charge, whilst emphasising tradition and continuity in Celtic warfare, assert that the charge was a modern innovation of the 1640s. However, it is possible to trace the origins of the tactic back further.

As discussed at the beginning of this chapter, the Celtic warrior society was composed of a small percentage of the warrior caste (known as 'Gentlemen'), and the remainder of the clan who were the tenants, sub-tenants and labourers of these gentlemen, known as 'ghillies'. Whilst it was the role of the Gentlemen to fight, the role of the ghillies was to back up their leader and provide fire support with arrows, stones or whatever came to hand.[15] Although no doubt expected to support their leaders once the fighting proper started, theirs was a fairly minor role. This position changed only slightly with the introduction of the firearm, for whilst the bow can be used to fire over the heads of the front ranks, the same is not possible with a musket which was, in addition, much slower to load and reload. As a result, the ghillies were now to have no alternative but to support physically the front ranks in the final charge to contact. It is perhaps useful at this point to compare the charge made by the troops under MacColla at Bendooragh in 1641 with that of earlier pre-firearms charges,

> If the Irish once saw a chance to close in it became a dance of death. Then they came on fast, with a hail of darts and loud shouts … If their opponents flinched and began to fly then they were lost … for the Irish were exceeding swift and terrible executioners.[16]

15. Heath, Ian, *Armies of the 16th Century* (Guernsey, 1997), p.72.
16. Heath, *The Irish Wars*, p.34.

Comparisons can, no doubt, be made with earlier European Celtic warfare.

The Salvo

The Salvo (drawing by Alan Turton).

An alternative to the counter-march system of fire control was the salvo, more commonly known in the British Isles as the 'Swedish Salvee'. Prior to contact with the enemy, the first three ranks of a regiment's musketeers would deliver into the enemy at short range a highly concentrated volley, as depicted above. Additionally, the salvo system, whilst allowing a unit to fire a concentrated volley, ensured that the remaining half of the musketeers would be uncommitted and held in reserve. Such tactics could only be used, however, by well-trained, disciplined troops.

Veteran English Parliamentarian troops under the command of Major General Lambert were to use such tactics to decisive effect against numerous 'Highland Charges' at Inverkeithing in 1651. In return for minimal losses on themselves, the English were able to inflict over 2,000 casualties, principally amongst the Highland clan regiments present. The salvo was also used to great effect by fellow veterans in Montrose's Irish Regiments who, through superior firepower, were able to overwhelm the poorly trained levies sent against them. The headgear depicted in the illustration is based upon archaeological discoveries made in Ireland.[17]

17. Dunlevy, Mairead, *Dress in Ireland* (London, 1989) pp.61-64.

5

Montrose's Regulars

The backbone of Montrose's armies throughout the Civil Wars was to be composed of regular troops. Amongst these regulars were the regiments which formed the 'Irish Brigade', under the leadership of Alastair MacColla. These troops have been often confused with Highland clansmen and are frequently portrayed as being equipped and fighting in the Highland style. Many modern writers seemingly support this traditional view.[1] In reality, however, they were mostly professionals, described by one contemporary source as, 'brockt up in West Flanderis, expert souldiouris'.[2] The Brigade was despatched to Scotland by the Earl of Antrim on behalf of the Irish Confederation, and the nature of its composition can be gleaned from the list of officers sent by Antrim to Ormond in 1644. 73 officers were named, with well over two-thirds of them having native Irish names, the rest having names that are English, Lowland Scottish or Highland in origin. It would not be unreasonable to assume that the troops under them would also have similar origins. Antrim further divides these forces into three regiments with companies, various officers, ensigns and non-commissioned officers attached.[3] This structure would seem to fit the model of most infantry formations that were to have been found in Western Europe at this time, and not that of a wild Gaelic mob.

Like their Scottish and English counterparts, the Irish were to be found in the military camps of Europe. The first Irish regiment to fight under the Spanish flag was raised by William Stanley in 1587, and from then on increasing numbers of Irish were to find themselves in French and Spanish service. As the Thirty Years' War drew on in Europe, the French in particular were to make extensive use of Irish troops. The French promoted Michael Wall of County Waterford, perhaps echoing David Leslie's achievement in the Swedish army, to army commander in 1639.[4] The outbreak of the Irish rebellion was to see considerable numbers of Irish troops, experienced in the latest military practices, return to Ireland.

The returning veterans, in addition to bringing military experience, also

1. Hill, p.48.
2. Spalding, p.385.
3. Danachair, Caoimhin O, 'Montrose's Irish Regiments', *Irish Sword*, Vol. 4, 959/60, pp.61-67.
4. Silke, John J., 'The Irish Abroad 1534-1691' in T.W. Moody, F.J. Bryne, F.X. Martin (eds.), *A New History of Ireland* Vol. 3 (Dublin, 1976), p.608.

brought back the latest ideas on how to support armies. After the initial series of uncoordinated attacks, the Catholic rebels had to create administrative structures with which they could support not only their new armies, but also at the same time procure monies and equipment. To this end a supreme council was established, along with an association, which was to resemble the English Parliament's regionalised war efforts. The role of the supreme council was to appoint military commands, build up war materials and create taxes with which to support the war effort.[5] The Confederacy was also able to gain support from abroad. France, Spain and the Papacy were able to contribute significant sums of money to the Catholic cause.[6] However, the bulk of finances was to be gathered from home. Using methods that proved to be very similar to the ones used by the warring factions in England, the Confederates cast the net far and wide. Supporters were asked to contribute, whilst merchants provided loans (considered by many to be an essential part of military funding). In addition, a mint was established at Waterford.[7] Traditional sources of revenue were used and others developed. Significant percentages of church tithes and freehold taxes were allocated to the support of the army. Excise duties were introduced and placed on liquor, tobacco and cattle.[8]

With the establishment of a financial infrastructure, the Confederates were able to develop a home armaments industry. Apart from over running production centres, such as furnaces and forges at Kilmacoe in County Wexford, they were able to establish their own industrial plant, such as the iron works at Artully in County Kerry.[9] To run the new plants and contribute their experience, foreign arms workers were sought out by the agents of the Confederacy to come to Ireland. The inducement of lifelong exemption and licence to name their own price for their products was used, and many were to arrive as early as 1642. Special efforts were made to attract foreign gunsmiths.[10]

Charles Tilly's statement, 'The state made war and war made the state' is certainly true of the Irish Catholic Confederation.[11] Geoffrey Parker, who by summarising Roberts' original thesis seemingly places the Confederation with the definition of the Military Revolution, further qualifies this statement:

'Roberts' military revolution dramatically accentuated the impact of war on society: the greater costs incurred, the greater damage inflicted, and the greater administrative challenge posed by the augmented armies made waging war far more of a burden and far more of a problem than ever previously, both for the civilian population and for their rulers.'[12]

Padraig Lenihan also contributes to the debate. He argues that if control

---

5. Edwards, pp.25-26.
6. Ibid., p.59.
7. Ibid., p.60.
8. Ibid., p.61.
9. Loeber, R. & G. Parker, 'The Military Revolution in Seventeenth-century Ireland', in J. Ohlmeyer (ed.), *Ireland from Independence to Occupation 1641-1660* (Cambridge 1995), p.75.
10. Edwards, p.89.
11. Leniham, Padraig, "'Celtic' Warfare in the 1640s', in John R. Young (ed.), *Celtic Dimensions of the British Civil Wars* (Edinburgh, 1997), p.116.
12. Parker, Geoffrey, *The Military Revolution: Military innovation and the rise of the West 1500-1800* (Cambridge 1988), pp.1-2. Lenihan, p.116.

Irish Musketeer in a 'Dungivern Jacket' and an Irish Montero. This musketeer has been able to obtain a full set of boxes, no doubt from one of the battlefields he has fought on. He retains his 'scian' single-edged Irish fighting knife. His woollen doublet is based upon the Dungiven site archaeological find of 1956. During the harsh winter of 1644-45 he possibly might have been fortunate enough to add a woollen cloak to his attire. His hat is an Irish interpretation of a Montero, the hat most closely associated with the contemporary European soldier of the day. Archaeological evidence from the period and earlier indicates that whilst many Irish were to adhere to traditional styles of headwear, others took to the fashion of their Continental peers by either direct import or local interpretation. (© Hugh Brogan)

of a standing army was a crucial determinant of seventeenth-century statehood, then the Irish Catholic Confederation can be seen as an emergent state because it was able to maintain quite large armies, despite its relatively limited financial structure.[13]

The modern nature of the Confederacy administration and war effort was also reflected in the equipping and organisation of its army. The 'traditionalist' school is led by writers such as James Hill, who claim that the sword was the principal weapon of the Celts, and that the charge was central to their tactics.[14] Closer examination, however, reveals a far greater degree of change and sophistication in military affairs. By the start of the 17th Century, the swordsman, whether in Celtic or Western European society, was rapidly becoming an anachronism. In the early 16th Century European armies, especially the Spanish, were to field considerable numbers of sword and buckler men. By the early 17th Century the swordsman had almost disappeared from the European battlefield.[15]

Like the longbow, a skilled swordsman could not have been produced in a matter of weeks and, like the longbow, its demise was hastened by the relative ease by which soldiers could be trained to use either pike or musket. During the forty years of peace that the British Isles enjoyed from 1603 to 1641, the only 'hands on' education in swordsmanship would have been available in Gaelic Scotland. Those Irishmen that flocked to the colours of the Confederacy in 1641 would have been the veterans of pike and shot warfare in Flanders and Germany, or were to be trained by these veterans in these modern methods. Like those veterans returning to Scotland in 1638, many Irish troops were to bring arms and equipment in lieu of pay with them on their return. Owen Roe O'Neil, who returned in 1642, was not only to bring three hundred commissioned and non-commissioned officers, veterans of Spanish service, but also a considerable amount of equipment and monies.[16] It is hard to imagine that these men would wish to disregard new skills and methods that were proven to work in favour of archaic traditions that were seen by many to be out of date by over forty years.

The output of the home industrial base certainly reflects the manner of weaponry made. Immediately after its capture by the Confederates, the ironworks at Lissan were immediately turned over to the production of pike heads. Special emphasis was placed on the home production of musket barrels and locks.[17] The inventory made by the Master Gunner of the Parliamentarian army of the captured Irish artillery puts forward the

13. Hill, p.1.
14. Heath, *Armies of the 16th Century*, p.131.
15. Ibid., p.131.
16. Wheeler, James Scott, *Cromwell in Ireland* (Dublin, 1999), p.17.
17. Edwards, p.89.

suggestion that the Confederacy had, at some time, even been able to establish a gun foundry.[18] The home industry was to become so well established that, after the Cessation of 1643, English Royalists were to place orders with the Irish arms industry.[19]

Export records are also able to build a profile of the equipment ordered by and issued to the Confederate armies. Early on in the rebellion, contact was made with friendly foreign powers and merchants and, as a result, the import of foreign weapons was soon well established. Shipments began to arrive in January 1642 and, by the end of February, the Venetian ambassador was able to report the large scale of deliveries to Ireland from the continent.[20] A sample delivery from Europe would be that made in October 1644 by Nicholas Everard and Jean de la Villette. Together they were to import 4,000 muskets, 1,000 pairs of pistols, 1,000 carbines, 20,000 lbs of match and 600 barrels of gunpowder.[21] So lucrative was the export of goods to the Confederacy that France, Spain and the United Provinces all attempted to solicit the business of the Confederates' agents and representatives.

Various Scottish regular units further supplemented the Irish regulars. Regiments such as Strathbogie had actually been in existence since the Bishops' Wars. A contingent of this regiment was described at the time as 'about 60 musketiers and pikoniers, with twa cullouris, ane drum, and ane bag pipe'.[22] They were trained by a professional soldier, Lieutenant Colonel Johnston, and were equipped with both musket and pike that the King had despatched to his Scottish supporters in the Bishops' Wars.[23] This unit amongst others (possibly even Highland clan regiments) was to benefit from the capture at Aberdeen in March 1645 of 1,800 muskets and pikes.[24] Montrose's attempts to raise significant numbers of Scottish regulars met with only limited success. To a greater extent this was his own fault. By failing to foster good relations with the various other Royalist rebel factions, such as the Gordons who dominated the north-east of Scotland, he was unable to consolidate control of an area long enough to raise and train viable numbers of regulars. An army of Scottish regulars would have gone a considerable distance to legitimise Montrose's cause. The use of Irish troops only served to alienate him from potential supporters.

The professionalism of Montrose's Irish regulars placed them in great demand with other rebel factions. As their numbers dwindled, Montrose was forced to become increasingly reliant on other regular troops, especially cavalry, that was to become more numerous as his 'Annus Mirabilis' wore on. The lack of regular cavalry prevented him from capitalising on his early victories in the autumn of 1644 and establishing himself in a commanding position in the Scottish lowlands a year earlier than he did. This problem was to be transformed by the defection to the Royalist cause of a regular cavalry unit led by Lord George Gordon. Like the Irish, these mounted troops have

18. Barratt, John, 'A Civil War Artillery Train', in *English Civil War Notes and Queries*, No. 32, p.14.
19. Edwards, p.189
20. Ibid., p.191
21. Ibid., p.193.
22. Spalding, p.349
23. Ibid., p.185
24. Ibid, p.453.

to a greater extent been 'romanticised' by various writers and bibliographers of Montrose.[25] However, from the descriptions of contemporary accounts, Gordon's horse and the other small troops of cavalry raised in support of the King's cause were seemingly trained and equipped in the orthodox 'harquebusier' style.[26] Though not numerically strong, cavalry were to play an increasingly significant role in Montrose's victories, particularly Auldearn, Alford and Kilsyth. At the later battle they were able to outnumber those fielded by the Government forces and played a key role in the Royalist rebel victory. Montrose's lack of political tact resulted in the loss of considerable numbers of Gordon's horse, when after the Battle of Kilsyth their use in the invasion of lowland Scotland would have been critical.

25. Wedgwood, C.V, *Montrose* (London, 1952), pp.86-87.
26. Wishart, George, *Memoirs of James, Marquess of Montrose, 1639-1650,* translated by G. Murdoch (London, 1893), p.88. See also Spalding, p.444.

6

Battlefield Performance

Battles and campaigns were not generally conclusive during the 17th Century. Jeremy Black argues that whilst the Swedes were able to inflict numerous defeats on their enemies, so did the French. Yet these victories were only short-term gains.[1] This was also to be the case in the English Civil War, as the battle of Marston Moor and the Lostwithiel Campaign, although possible 'knock-out' blows, did not bring a rapid conclusion to the war.[2] The Marquess of Montrose's campaign was to be no exception for, although he was able to inflict numerous severe reverses on his opponents, after just a little over a year he had little or nothing to show for the sacrifices made by him or his men.

During the course of the First Civil War, Montrose and his army were to take part in eight major actions. He was to be victorious at Tippermuir (1 September 1644), Aberdeen (13 September 1644), Fyvie Castle (28 October 1644), Inverlochy (2 February 1645), Auldearn (9 May 1645), Alford (2 July 1645) and Kilsyth (15 August 1645). His victorious campaign, together with his military and political creditability, ended with his defeat at Philiphaugh (13 September 1645).

Note: in the text below, the term 'regular' refers to those troops who were equipped and fought in a contemporary European manner and includes those Highlander units who followed these trends. 'Irregular' refers to Highland troops who still fought in a traditional Gael manner.

Tippermuir 1 September 1644[3]

1,500 Irish regulars
500 Lord Kilpoints Regiment
1,000 Highland clansmen

Regular troops 66%

1. Black, Jeremy, *A Military Revolution? Military Change and European Society 1550-1800* (London, 1991), p.13.
2. The writer is aware that this can be seen as a contentious issue.
3. Gordon, Patrick of Ruthven, *History of Scots Affairs* (Aberdeen, 1844), p.74. See also Wishart, pp.56-57. For further discussion on and a greater analysis of the battles fought by this army, see Stuart Reid's *The Campaigns of Montrose* (Edinburgh, 1990).

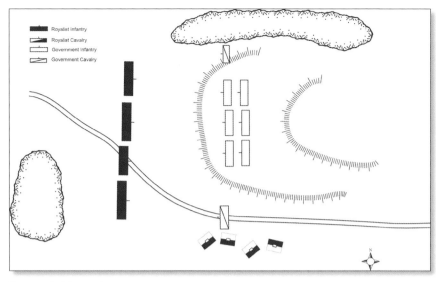

Tippermuir, 1 September 1644. (George Anderson)

Irregular troops 33%

Following some skirmishing between Government and Irish musketeers, a general advance was called by Montrose. In the centre, an intense firefight was won by MacColla's Irish, who promptly sent their raw opponents running from the field. On the Royalist right, led by Montrose, the clansman of Atholl failed to stop a cavalry charge with a volley, but following up with a charge they were able to put both Government horse and foot to flight. The remaining Government troops facing the Royalist right seemed to have been swept away in the general collapse of their army.

Aberdeen 13 September 1644[4]

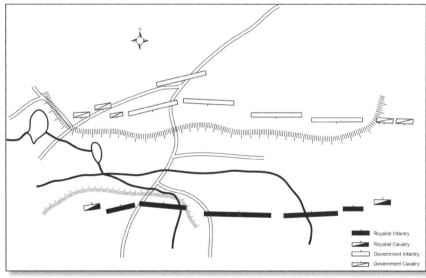

Aberdeen, 13 September 1644. (George Anderson)

1,500 Irish regulars
80 cavalry

Regular troops 100%

The action began with skirmishing around the Justice Mills. The Royalists were able to drive out the Government musketeers stationed there, only to be attacked in turn by supporting cavalry. Whilst fighting was developing around the mill, Government cavalry charged O'Cahan's Irish infantry. Opening their ranks, the Irish infantry let the cavalry through and fired a volley into their backs. The survivors were finished off by the Royalist cavalry led by Nathaniel Gordon.

With similar activity happening on the opposite flank, Montrose ordered a general advance of his centre which, after a prolonged fight, saw a general collapse of the Government army.

---

4. Gordon, p.81; Wishart, pp.66-67.

Fyvie Castle 28 October 1644[5]

800 Irish regulars
200 Scottish regulars
300 Highland clansmen

Regular troops 66%
Irregular troops 33%

Fighting a defensive action amongst enclosures and hilly and wooded terrain, Montrose and a reduced Royalist army hold against forces led by the Marquess of Argyle for three days. Despite some fighting on the first day, Argyle retires due to the lack of supplies.

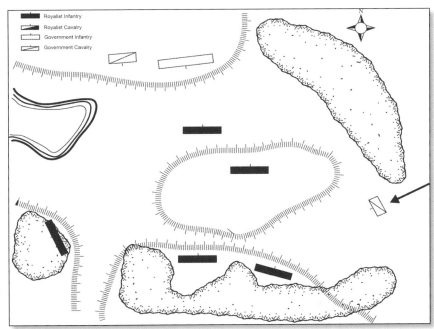

Fyvie Castle, 28 October 1644.
(George Anderson)

Inverlochy 2 February 1645[6]

1,000 Irish regulars
500 Highland clansmen

Regular troops 66%
Irregular troops 33%

Following an arduous route march over the Highlands in the middle of a harsh winter, the Royalists immediately went over to the attack. With Irish forming the wings and the western clans forming the centre, a general advance was ordered. The Irish on the wings made contact first with a volley at very close range, following up with charging with sword and pike. The Government centre, seeing the collapse of the wings, followed suit when charged by the Highlanders

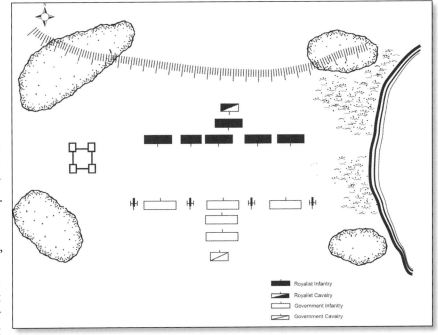

Inverlochy, 2 February 1645.
(George Anderson)

---

5. Gordon, p.81.
6. Spalding, p.444; Stevenson, p.156.

commanded by Montrose in person.

Auldearn 9 May 1645[7]

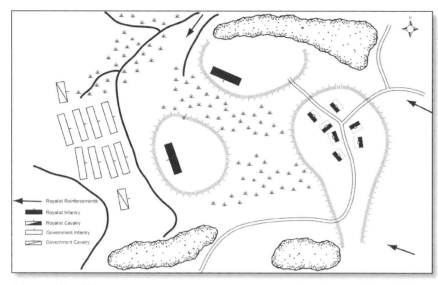

Auldearn, 9 May 1645.
(George Anderson)

800 Irish regulars
1,000 Scottish regulars
200 Scottish regular cavalry
200 Highland clansmen

Regular troops 80%
Irregular troops 20%

Surprised by a rapid advance by a Government army led by Sir John Hurry, MacColla fought a desperate delaying action with his bodyguard and whatever troops he could gather around him. Eventually he was driven off his hilltop position into the closed environment of Auldern village. Here a stalemate ensued as the Government troops struggled to use superior numbers to force their way into the village, and counter-attacks led by MacColla faltered as they struggled uphill.

This impasse, however, enabled the Royalist army to rally and form up. Counter-attacks by regular infantry and cavalry into the flanks of the Government forces ensured victory.

Alford 2 July 1645[8]

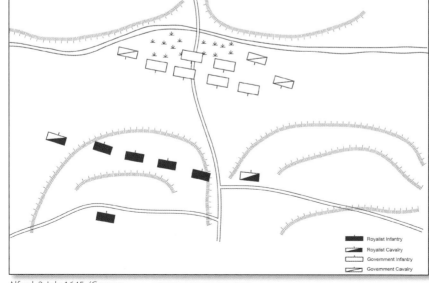

Alford, 2 July 1645. (George Anderson)

600 Irish regulars
700 Scottish regulars
200 Scottish regular cavalry
600 Highland clansmen

Regular troops 66%
Irregular troops 33%

Both armies deployed in the conventional manner of the

7. Gordon, pp.122-130; Spalding, p.473.
8. Gordon, pp.129-130; Wishart, p.109.

period – infantry in the centre and cavalry on the wings. Gordon's cavalry on the Royalist right, supported by elements of Irish infantry, defeated the Government horse opposing them. They then wheeled behind the Government infantry in the centre to hit the rear of the enemy horse fighting on the left. The infantry centre of the Government force was then overwhelmed by combined assaults of Royalist infantry and cavalry attacks. The French victory at Rocroi was achieved by a similar cavalry manoeuvre.

Kilsyth 15 August 1645[9]

600 Irish regulars
800 Scottish regulars
600 Scottish regular cavalry
1,600 Highland clansmen

Regular troops 60%
Irregular troops 40%

Having detected the Royalist camp, Government forces under the command of William Baillie attempted a flank march trying to gain higher

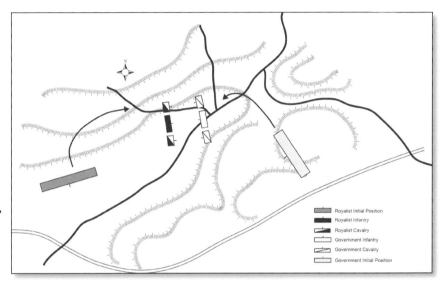

Kilsyth, 15 August 1645.
(George Anderson)

ground. Clashes soon broke out as the Covenanter army made their flank march, with the left wing of Baillie's force, now the rear of the march column, attacking the Highlander infantry occupying cottages on Montrose's left flank, and the cavalry on the Government right wing, now the vanguard, attacking the Royalist cavalry. Other Covenant and Royalist units joined the fray, acting without orders. Montrose seized the unexpected opportunity, and sent his cavalry and Highlanders against the now disrupted Covenant column. The mass of the Royalist infantry subsequently joined in the attack. Baillie's army soon started to disintegrate; the veterans were able to make their way from the battlefield in some semblance of order, but the levies broke and ran.

---

9.   Gordon, p.136; Wishart, pp.138-143.

Philiphaugh 13 September 1645[10]

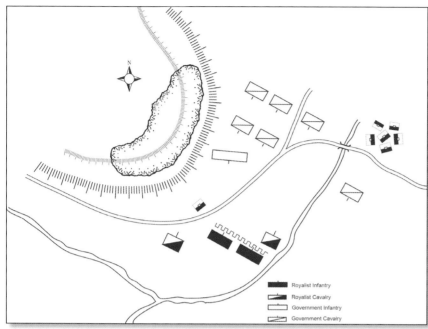

Philiphaugh, 13 September
1645. (George Anderson)

500 Irish regulars
1,000 cavalry

Regular troops 100%

Montrose, having advanced to the Scottish borders with few regulars, was able to recruit large numbers of poorly-led and untried cavalry. Showing the same disregard for intelligence and scouting as he did at Auldearn, both he and his small army were pounced on by a large force of veteran cavalry from the Scottish Government army operating in England. The Royalists were overthrown and scattered in very short order.

Having examined how the army was equipped, and how it complied with contemporary European thinking, it is necessary to see how its individual components used these new ideas and techniques to achieve dominance on the battlefield.

Montrose's battles, with the exception of Auldearn (a bungled ambush of Montrose by the Government general Hurry), and Philiphaugh (not so much a battle, as a one-sided mopping-up operation), were typical set piece actions where one or both of the opposing sides would advance to contact.

The Marquess's battles can be divided into three parts – advance to contact with a firefight, hand-to-hand combat and final stage

During this period, when armies advanced to small arms range and contact, one of two sequences occurred – either a single volley pre-empted an attack with musket butt and pike, or a protracted firefight followed by eventual hand-to-hand action.

The typical scenario of events at this, the opening stage of a battle, would see numbers of musketeers being fed into a firing line in order to drive an enemy unit or line from a position. If these were unable to do so then the whole unit would be brought up to settle the issue at close quarters. Musket fire was on the whole a very ineffective method of creating mass casualties. This is supported by various eyewitness accounts. Major-General Morgan, in

10. Gordon, pp.156-159; Wishart, p.145.

his narrative of the Battle of the Dunes in 1658, wrote of Spanish musketry; "the enemy poured a volley of shot into one of our battalions, wounded three or four and one dropped". A second firing was to produce poorer results – "the enemy poured in another volley of shot into another of our battalions; and wounded two or three".[11] It should be remembered that the Spanish troops the English were fighting were not poorly trained conscripts, but time-served veterans of the Army of Flanders. Arguably, the main aim of the musket firefight was to intimidate, disorder and suppress one's opponents by a force of will and a sheer volume of fire, not by casualties alone.[12]

The experience of the Irish and Scottish regulars in Montrose's army during this phase of a battle would seem to differ very little from those of troops elsewhere in Europe. At Tippermuir, Gordon describes the Irish regiments as advancing and, 'at the first encounter with the Irishes played upon with hott alarums and continuall fyre'.[13] This account would suggest that an extensive and long drawn-out firefight took place. A similar event occurs a fortnight later at the Battle of Aberdeen, where the Royalist centre once again advanced towards the enemy, for as Gordon describes, 'it was disputed hard for a long space'.[14]

Whilst most of the Government armies would have used the counter-march method of fire control described earlier, there is evidence that the Irish used the salvo method. At Inverlochy in February 1645, Montrose was to order his regular musketeers on the flanks of his army 'not to giue fyre till he gaue it in there breastes, and this course in the right wing he rightly obserues also; and thus patiently receaueing there shote without giueing fyre, till they fyred there beardes, both wings make a cruell hauoke of the enemies'.[15] In order to maximise the effect of their combined firepower, the Royalist musketeers, who at Inverlochy would have been nearly all Irish, would have held their fire until they were only a few feet away from the Covenant troops. At such close range with the optimum number of firearms possible, even accounting for the inadequacies of the musket, such a volley would have been devastating.

The salvo was a product of the 17th Century's 'Military Revolution'. Although possibly Dutch in origin, used as early the Battle of Nieuwport in 1600, its chief exponent was the Swedish army of Gustavus Adolphus. Sir James Turner, a Scottish soldier in the employ of the Swedish king, was to describe the salvo or 'salvee' as thus:

> For thereby you pour as much lead in your enemies bosom at one time as you do the other way at two several times [i.e. the counter march system[, and thereby you do them more mischief, you quail, daunt, and astonish them three times more, for one long and continual crack of thunder is more terrible and dreadful to mortals than ten interrupted and several ones.[16]

11. Morgan, Sir Thomas, 'A true and just relation of Major-General Sir Thomas Morgan's progress … as it was delivered by the General himself' in *English Civil War Notes and Queries* issue 34, p.6.
12. Peachey, Stuart, *The Mechanics of Infantry Combat in The First Civil War* (Bristol, 1992), p.20.
13. Gordon, p.74; Reid, *The Campaigns of Montrose*, p.53.
14. Gordon, p.82.
15. Ibid, p.101.
16. Parker, Geoffrey, *The Thirty Years War* (London, 1984), p.185.

Turner is able to convey the tremendous disruption, if not casualties, caused by a well-executed salvo. This method of fire control was not unknown in Scotland. *The Swedish Intelligencer* was able to report a very clear description of how the salvo was carried out by other Scots in the Swedish service:

> The Scots ordering themselves in severall small battagliaes, about 6 or 700 in a body, presently now double their rankes, making their files then but 3 deepe, the discipline of the King of Sweden beeng to march aboue 6 deepe. This done, the formost ranke falling on their knees; the second stooping forward; and the third ranke standing right up, and all giuing fire together; they powerd so much lead at one instant in amongst the enemies horse that their ranckes were much broken by it.[17]

It was knowledge of the Swedish salvo which helped influence some of Montrose's tactical decisions. *The History of the King's Affairs in Scotland under the Conduct of the Marquess of Montrose* comments that at one battle:

> Montrose perceiving the great strength of the enemy … he caused his army to be drawne out to as open an order as could be possible, and makes his files onely three deep. He commands the ranks all to discharge at once, those in the first ranke kneeling, in the second stooping, and in the hindmost where he placed the tallest men upright.[18]

Jeremy Black argues that experienced and well-motivated troops during the era of the Military Revolution usually carried the day, and during this stage of a battle discipline and good training were vital.[19] Poorly trained or easily intimidated by superior firepower could easily reduce a body of troops into chaos, as was often the case of the Government levies who fought against Montrose. One account of a unit, who had gotten the worse of a firefight during the war in Scotland, reads:

> … a Lieutenant giving out the unhappy word of counter march, all the men possessed as it were of a panic fear, began somewhat confusedly to march back; but they were so much amazed with a second shout given by the rebels, who seeing them in disorder followed close on, as notwithstanding that they had gotten into a ground of great advantage, they could not be persuaded to stand a charge, but betook themselves to their heels, and so the rebels fell sharply on, as their manner is, upon the execution.[20]

At some point during the exchange of missile fire, one side would begin to suffer from a gradual loss of cohesion and order. This could be from a variety of reasons; poor training combined with lack of experience under fire, or the disorder brought on by being under fire. It was at this point that Montrose's

---

17. Firth, C.H, *Cromwell's Army* (London, 1902), p.97.
18. Ibid., p.98.
19. Black, p.10.
20. Leniham, p.127.

infantry would endeavour to take advantage of any disorder, and attempt to close with their opponents in order to engage in hand-to-hand combat.

The advance to contact usually followed the discharge of a volley. The Swedes introduced this aggressive infantry tactic to Europe in the early stages of the Thirty Years War. Traditionally the pike was the melee-winning weapon, but the reality was very different. The Swedes would frequently discharge muskets at point blank range, before charging into a confused enemy with sword and musket butt.[21] This new tactic was soon to gain popularity throughout the rest of Europe, and the British Isles were to be no exception. The Royalist regulars had no sooner fired by salvo at Aberdeen then they attacked the Covenant infantry, 'with there swords assailed both horse and foote men so desperately as they first fell in confusion and disorder'.[22] This same procedure happens again at Aberdeen: 'Scarce had he [Montrose] given the word when they charged, and hurling them [the Government troops] into utter confusion, put them to utter rout.'[23] A much clearer example of the charge to contact is described by Gordon of Ruthven of the Irish assault at Inverlochy, ' ... both wings make a cruell hauoke of the enemies; leaping in amongst them with there swords ... they quickly put them to disorder, and disperses them ower all the fieldes.'[24]

This practice was widespread elsewhere in the British Isles during this period. Two occasions (albeit of Royalist experiences) illustrate this tactic as popular amongst other veteran soldiers. The first is recorded by Sir Walter Slingsby's account of Royalist musketeers in action at the Battle of Cheriton (29 March 1644),

> ... the foote keeping theire ground in a close body, not firing til within two pikes length, and then three rankes att a time, after turning up the butt end of theire muskets, charging theire pikes, and standing close, preserv'd themselues, and slew many of the enemy.[25]

The second event, the Battle of Naseby (14 June 1645), was recorded by Sir Edmund Walker and Clarendon. Walker, at the time the King's secretary, describes the Royalist infantry assault as:

> 'Presently our Forces (of foot) advanced up the hill, the Rebells only discharging five Pieces at them, but over shot them, and so did their Musquetiers at them. The Foot on either side hardly saw each other until they were with Carabine shot, and so made only one volley; ours falling in with Sword and butt end of Musquet did nitable execution; so much as I saw their Colours fall, and their Foot in great Disorder ... "[26]

The New Model Army, as recorded by Fairfax's Secretary John Rushworth were to reply also with salvo.

21. Brzezinski, Richard, *Lützen 1632* (Oxford, 2001), p.21.
22. Gordon, p.74.
23. Wishart, p.68.
24. Gordon, p.101. Author's italics.
25. Adair, John, *Cheriton 1644* (Kineton, 1973), p.131.
26. Reid, Stuart, *Gunpowder Triumphant* (Leigh on Sea, 1987), p.40.

Clarendon, (albeit not an eyewitness) further qualifies this with his own account:

> The King's foot, according to their usual custom, fell to with their swords and butt ends of their muskets, with which they did very notable execution, and put the enemy into great disorder and confusion.[27]

The increasingly aggressive tactics of infantry during this period were to make them less vulnerable to cavalry. Musketeers, who were traditionally weak against mounted unless supported by bodies of pike, were able to fend for themselves. The Duke of York, the future James II, wrote of an event at the Battle of the Dunes (14 June 1658):

> 'Tis very observable that when we had broken into this battalion, and were gott amongst them, not so much as one single man of them asked for quarter, or threw down his arms, but every one defended himself to the last; so that we ran as great a danger by the butt of their muskets as by the volley which they had given us. And one of them had infallibly knocked mee off my horse, if I had not prevented him when he was just ready to have discharged his blow by a stroke I gave with my sword over the face, which laid him along upon the ground.[28]

The Duke, whilst describing part of a battle on the continent, could have easily have been describing the action of the Royalist Irish infantry who were themselves attacked by cavalry at Aberdeen in 1644.

> Craigieware fell nixt to charge with his troupe … .for the Irishes throw whom he charged, being so well trained men as the world could afford no better, oppins there rankes receiueing him, and close againe immediately by commande … and then on all quarters giues fyre vpon. Few or non of his troupe went backe that durst wenter with hm …[29]

Frequently posted on the flanks of the Royalist army, the regular infantry acted in tandem and in support of the cavalry. On more than one occasion regular infantry was to intervene on behalf of the Royalist cavalry. At the Battle of Alford, Irish infantry intervened when the Royalist right cavalry wing began to collapse whilst under pressure and help to rout the opposing cavalry.[30] Gordon describes the action as, ' … Colonell M'Lachlen fell to worke with there horses, whereof there ware not ten or twelfe lamed when they tooke them to flight.'[31] The practice of supporting the cavalry wings with small detachments of infantry was by the 1640s common practice on

27. Hyde, Edward, Earl of Clarendon, *The History of the Great Rebellion,* Roger Lockyer (ed.) (Oxford, 1970), pp.269-270. This account is more than likely based on Walker's.

28. Firth, p.106.

29. Gordon, p.82. Government foot at Kilsyth also practised this 'anti-cavalry' manoeuvre – see Reid, *The Campaigns of Montrose,* p.146.

30. Reid, Stuart, *The Campaigns of Montrose* (Edinburgh, 1990), p.130. See also Paterson, Raymond Campbell, *A Land Afflicted, Scotland and the Covenanter Wars 1638-1690* (Edinburgh 1998), p.97.

31. Gordon, Book III, p.130.

the Continent, and is once again frequently attributed to the Swedes. [32] This tactic, whilst being used by the Scottish Royalists, also saw extensive use by other armies in the British Isles. Prince Rupert, himself a veteran of the European wars, introduced integrated cavalry and musketeer wings on several occasions, notably Marston Moor and Naseby.[33]

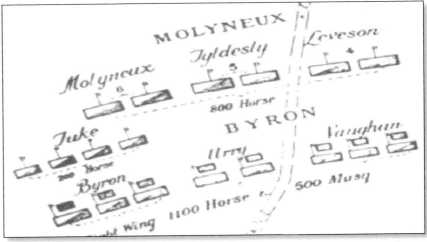

Rupert's deployment of musketeer detachments (small blocks behind the cavalry of Byron, Hurry and Vaughan) can be clearly seen in this Victorian version of Sir Bernard de Gomme's plan of Marston Moor.

The presence of cavalry in what has traditionally been seen as a Highland host army, must surely question the nature of such an army with little or no tradition of a cavalry arm. Cavalry was to play an increasingly dominant role in Montrose's battles, and at Auldearn, Alford and Kilsyth made significant contributions to the Royalist victories. Tactical doctrine in the mid-17th Century was divided between the Dutch and Swedish schools. Dutch doctrine emphasised the use of firepower to break up an enemy advance, before responding with a counter attack. The Swedish doctrine relied on the shock of impact, a rapid advance to melee, using both pistol and sword for combat.[34]

During the early stages of the war, Parliament's cavalry on the whole adopted the Dutch methods whilst the King's cavalry, possibly lacking the equipment and resources for a sustained firearms duel, opted for the rapid advance to contact advocated by the Swedes.

Towards the end of the war, with both sides having gained considerable experience, equipment and tactics were to become very similar. A contemporary was to describe these developments as:

> Those troops that are to give the first charge … are to be at their close order … then drawing neere the Enemy, they are to take forth one of their Pistols out of their holsters … firing as before … having thus fired, the troops are to charge the Enemy in full career.[35]

Montrose's cavalry were no exception. Indeed, Lord Gordon, colonel of the largest cavalry unit in Montrose's army, had seen service in the French forces, arguably the inheritors of the Swedish tactics. During the campaign's early battles, the small numbers of Royalist cavalry were, with infantry support, able to hold their own. By the middle of 1645, now greatly increased

32. Brzezinski. Richard, *The Army of Gustavus Adolphus (2): Cavalry*, (London, 1993), pp.33-34.
33. Young, Peter, *Marston Moor 1644 – The Campaign and the Battle* (Kineton, 1970), p.104.
34. Tincey, John, *Soldiers of the English Civil War (2): Cavalry*, (London, 1990), pp.16-18.
35. Vernon, John, *The Young Horse-man, or the Honest Plain-Dealing Cavalier*, John Tincey (ed.) (Frome, 1993), p.86.

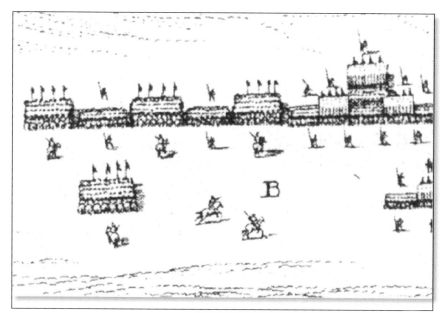

A contemporary depiction of a Swedish cavalry flank from the *Theatrum Europaeum* III. Small detachments of infantry are clearly to be seen deployed between the regiments of horse. To the right of the horse is a scarce depiction of the 'Swedish Brigade', a formation rarely used during the life time of Gustavus Adolphus, and less so after his death. By deploying bodies of musketeers with his horse, Montrose, like the Swedish King would have hoped to, "easily push off the enemy's attacking cavalry and keep them back."

in numbers they were able to dominate the battlefield and at Auldearn and Kilsyth were able to strike the knockout blow.

Gordon's account of the Royalist cavalry under the command of Lord Gordon leaves no doubt to the aggressive tactics used:

My lord Gordon by this time charges the left wing, and with a new form of fight, for he discharges all shooting of pistols and carrabines, only with ther swords to charge quyht throwgh ther enemies … my lord Gordon charges with soundly with swords only, as if they scorned to be resisted; they had all sworn to go throw or dye. [36]

Having cleared the Government cavalry from the field, the Royalist horse was promptly to smash into the flank of the opposing infantry centre. Similar Swedish tactics were employed again at Kilsyth:

The horse troupes [of the Government army] adwanceth befor the foot to gaine a high ground; but was sharply encounterd by adjutant Gordoune, who was send befor the armie to gaine that same high ground, and charged them so soundly as he beat them back againe within the bodie of ther foote … [37]

---

36. Gordon, pp.125-126.
37. Gordon, pp.139-140.

Conclusion

Montrose won battles because his was a better trained, officered and handled army. The Government armies sent against them, whilst staffed with some experienced officers, were frequently hampered by poor quality levies and insubordinate officers. The committee of civilian advisors, which was invariably attached to government forces and whose authority was frequently to overrule that of the army's military leaders, also led to significant problems.

Most of the troops serving in the Royalists' Scottish armies were regular soldiers, equipped with pike and musket; these included a significant numbers of Highlanders. It was these regular troops who formed the majority of Montrose's armies and did the bulk of the fighting. Those Highlanders, equipped and fighting in the traditional tribal fashion, were only sent into battle once the back of cohesive resistance had been broken. The clansman was adequate only for consolidating a victory once others had achieved it. On occasions when they took it upon themselves to initiate offensive actions with little forethought or preparation, they would find themselves in serious difficulties. At Montrose's last victory at Kilsyth, large numbers of Highlanders rapidly advanced towards the enemy's front line, only to be pinned down and suppressed by a heavy volume of musket fire. Despite suffering few casualties, they refused to advance again until rescued by regular cavalry. Undisciplined and poorly equipped, with only a front rank of 'Gentlemen' having any martial prowess, the Scottish Highlander was of only marginal military value. Their usefulness was limited to raiding, plundering and skirmishing.

Prior to the defection of a regular cavalry unit in February 1645, Montrose's army was infantry-based; after that date it was a conventional army that would not have looked out of place on the battlefields of Europe. During the English Civil Wars, numerous other provincial armies would field significant numbers of peasant levies. Lord Fairfax's Yorkshire Parliamentarian army at Adwalton Moor (30 June 1643) had a large contingent of 'club men', described as: ' … fit to do execution upon a flying enemy … ' Their performance was as abysmal as their Highland counterparts, for they fled as the first cannon were fired. Other largely irregular armies, such as the various 'club men' contingents that were raised towards the end of the First Civil War, were all to receive short shrift from regular troops. The changes in military affairs that occurred during the 17th Century not only produced the professional regular soldier, but also created an ever-widening gulf between him and the part-time amateur.

Postscript

On the morning of 16 April 1746, in an action lasting little over an hour, the Highland clansmen were comprehensively defeated for the last time by professional regular troops at Culloden Moor. That afternoon, whilst searching the battlefield, over 3,000 firelock muskets with bayonets fixed were found, in addition to 500 cwt of musket balls. Less than 200 broadswords were discovered. The transition that had started in the early part of the last century was by this time almost complete. The next occasion on which the Scottish highlander was to fight in any significant numbers was in the red coat of the British army.

Appendix

Eyewitness Accounts of Montrose's Battles

I – George Wishart's account of the battles of Tippermuir, Aberdeen and Auldearn[1]

Having fled the rise of the Covenanters, Wishart was appointed to the afternoon lectureship at St Nicholas Church, Newcastle. With the surrender of the city to the Scots in October 1644, Wishart, along with other prisoners, was sent to Edinburgh and imprisoned in the Tolbooth, where he was to remain for nearly a year. Following Montrose's victory at Kilsyth in August 1645, he was released. He joined the Royalist army and was appointed chaplain to Montrose, now the acting governor general of Scotland.

From this point onwards, Wishart is with the Royalist army, was an eyewitness to the campaign and was able to get first hand accounts of what had happened previously in 1644 and the early part of 1645. Following Montrose into exile, Wishart started to write his famous *The Memoirs of James Marquess of Montrose* whilst at the Royalist enclave in The Hague, and finished it sometime in October 1647.

Although very likely to be present at Philiphaugh, he was not present at any other of the major battles. His account of the campaign and, in particular, the battle of Auldearn, where he was very forgiving of Montrose's lack of preparedness, has influenced many later historians and writers.

Tippermuir

Wishart's description of the battle, in particular the fight in the infantry centre, was collected in the main from Montrose, who was fighting on the right wing of the Royalist army, and thus saw little of no fighting in the centre. His account of the battle is very different from that of Patrick Gordon of Ruthven, whose account is based upon those of Montrose, MacColla and other veterans of the battle.

Montrose learned that the Covenanters had gathered in great numbers at Perth

---

1. Taken from *Memoirs of James, Marquess of Montrose 1639-1650* (translated by Murdoch & Simpson, London, 1893).

[the second city of Scotland, next to Edinburgh] and were there awaiting his descent from Athole. As he knew that Argyll with his army was close on his heels, to avoid being hemmed in between two armies, he determined to march on Perth, and either force the enemy to fight, or take the town and reduce it to obedience. Accordingly he advanced three miles from Buchanty, and, after a very brief halt to rest his men, resumed his march at early dawn. Not more than three miles from Perth he saw the enemy drawn up for battle on a broad open plain called Tippermuir. They were commanded by Lord Elcho who had no great reputation as a soldier. With him were the Earl of Tullibardine and Lord Drummond, the latter, it was reported, against his will, he and all his father's family being at heart favourable to the King.

There were also very many knights, of whom the most distinguished officer was Sir James Scott, who had served with credit in the Venetian army. Their forces consisted of 6,000 foot and 700 horse and, trusting to their numbers, they had already in anticipation devoured their enemy. It was Sunday the 1st of September, and their ministers were specially charged to encourage the soldiers in their sermons and animate them for battle by reminding them of their (so-called) Holy Covenant. And, to give them their due, they performed their part stoutly at the expense of their lungs, promising them in the name of God Almighty an easy and bloodless victory. Nay, one of them, Frederick Carmichael, esteemed by the ignorant people a man of great learning and holiness, did not hesitate to declare in his discourse, 'If ever God spoke certain truth out of my mouth, in His name I promise you to-day a certain victory.'

Having finished their devotions duly, as they thought, they drew up their army in order of battle. Elcho himself commanded the right wing; Sir James Scott, the left, and the Earl of Tullibardine, the centre. The cavalry were posted on the wings, by which they confidently expected on such open ground to surround the enemy. When Montrose saw the superior numbers of the enemy, and especially their strength in horse, as he himself had not a single trooper, and not more than three horses altogether, lean, sorry jades, he had reason to fear he might be surrounded, and attacked in front, rear, and flank. He therefore extended his line as much as possible, in files only three deep, with orders to discharge all at once, those in the front rank kneeling, the second stooping, and the rear rank, in which he placed his tallest men, standing erect. They were to waste no powder, of which they stood in great need, and not to fire a single shot till face to face with the enemy; then after one discharge, to fall on bravely with drawn swords and muskets clubbed; and the enemy, he assured them confidently, would never stand their charge.

Montrose himself took command of the right wing, facing Sir James Scott. The left he assigned to Lord Kilpont, and the centre to Macdonald with his Irish. This was an excellent arrangement, for the Irish, who had neither long pikes nor swords, if placed on the wings would have been exposed to the enemy's cavalry.

Montrose had sent Drummond, Lord Maderty's eldest son, a very accomplished young nobleman, to the leaders of the enemy, to declare, in his name, that he, as well as his royal master, whose commission he bore, had the utmost abhorrence of shedding his countrymen's blood, and most earnestly desired a bloodless victory.

Such a victory both armies might gain if they would return to their duty

1. Irish Ensign. (Photo: Dave Swift/Interpreter: Sebastian Stock © Claíomh 2014)

2. MacColla Lifeguard. (Photo: Niamh O'Rourke/ Interpreter: Dave Swift © Claíomh 2014)

See Colour Plate Commentaries for full captions

PLATE B

1. Irish Musketeer. (Painting by Anthony Barton, © Helion & Company Limited)

2. 'Regular' Pikeman. (Painting by Anthony Barton, © Helion & Company Limited)

See Colour Plate Commentaries for full captions

PLATE C

'Regular' Cavalry Trooper. (Painting by Anthony Barton, © Helion & Company Limited)

See Colour Plate Commentaries for full captions

Montrose's Irish Brigade at the Battle of Aberdeen, 13 September 1644. (Painting by Peter Dennis, © Helion & Company Limited)

See Colour Plate Commentaries for full captions

See Colour Plate Commentaries for full captions

Highlanders. (Painting by Anthony Barton, © Helion & Company Limited)

See Colour Plate Commentaries for full captions

See Colour Plate Commentaries for full captions

PLATE F

1. Irish Pikeman in Scottish dress. (Photo: Dave Swift/
Interpreter: Hanno Conring © Claíomh 2014)

2. Irish Musketeer. (Photo: Dave Swift/
Interpreter: Marcus Byrne © Claíomh 2014)

See Colour Plate Commentaries for full captions

and allegiance without the hazard of war. He was neither covetous of honours for himself nor envious of other men's preferment, and had no designs against the lives of his fellow countrymen. All he desired was that in God's name they would at length give ear to sounder counsels, and trust to the clemency, faith, and protection of so good a King.

Hitherto His Majesty had fully complied with all the demands of his Scotch subjects, both in civil and religious matters, though to the very great prejudice of his royal prerogative, and was still ready, like a most indulgent father, though provoked by unspeakable injuries, to embrace his penitent children with open arms. If, notwithstanding, they persisted in rebellion, he called God to witness that their stubbornness forced him into the present strife.

To this they made no reply. Contrary to the law of nations, they seized the envoy, who had undertaken that office solely out of love to his country, and sent him under guard to Perth, to be imprisoned like a malefactor, impiously vowing that after their victory they would cut off his head. But God was more merciful, and provided otherwise than they intended for the safety of this noble and accomplished man.

As soon as they were within cannon-shot the enemy, under Lord Drummond, sent out some picked men to skirmish with Montrose and harass his line. To check them he despatched a small body, who at the first onset threw them into disorder, routed them, and drove them back in panic on their own line.

Montrose seized the decisive moment to charge; nothing could animate his men and strike terror into the enemy more effectually than an immediate attack, while they were still confused and dismayed at this first blow, before they had time to rally or recover courage.

With a loud cheer he hurled his whole line upon them. The enemy discharged their cannon, which were planted in front, but at such a distance, that they produced more noise than execution.

They then advanced, and their horse moved forward to attack. But Montrose's men, though their powder was spent, and few of them were armed with pikes or even swords, received them boldly with such weapons as fell to hand, namely, stones, no less, of which they poured in heavy volleys with such force and spirit that they compelled them to sound a retreat and trouble them no more. The Irish and Highlanders, in gallant rivalry, behaved with the utmost courage, and pressed so hard on their retreat that at last they broke and fled. On the right wing the engagement lasted longer.

Here James Scott for some time made a desperate effort to gain the higher ground. But Montrose's men, who were superior in strength of body, and especially in speed and agility, seized the position.

Then the Athole men charged down with drawn claymores, and, unchecked by a hail of bullets from the musketeers, they closed with them, slashing and cutting down all before them. Unable to stand the shock, the enemy at last fairly fled away. Most of the cavalry saved themselves by the speed of their horses, but among the foot there was a very great slaughter, as the conquerors pursued them for six or seven miles. Two thousand Covenanters are said to have been slain and a larger number captured. Some of them took the oath of service and enlisted with the victor; but nearly all of them broke their word and deserted. The rest were set at liberty on parole never afterwards to fight against the King or his generals. On the same day Montrose took Perth, without inflicting any damage, though most of the inhabitants had fought against him in the battle. By this act of signal mercy he hoped to win them to the King, the sole end and aim of all his plans.

Aberdeen

Wishart's account of Aberdeen, apart from the famous anecdote of the Irish soldier who loses a leg, describes Montrose's use of the Swedish practice of supporting cavalry with musketeers, 'his most active musketeers and archers, who in agility and speed were almost as good as horsemen'.

… Meantime he [Montrose] received intelligence that Commissioners of the Covenanters, with Lord Burleigh, their chief and president, lay at Aberdeen with an army, and were labouring hard, by entreaties, bribes, or force of arms, to win over the northern parts, on which Montrose chiefly relied. He resolved to drive them out at once, before Argyll could join them with his army, and hastened thither by forced marches. Seizing the bridge of Dee, he approached the city, and found the enemy drawn out before it in battle array. Lord Burleigh commanded 2,000 foot, and 500 horse which he stationed on the wings. He occupied a strong position and, with his cannon well placed in front, was ready for battle.

Montrose's army numbered only 1,500 foot, for Kilpont's men had gone to escort the body of their dead leader to his parents, and most of the Athole men, after the victory at Perth, had gone off laden with booty to their own country, which was not far off.

His horse, numbering only forty-four, he divided and posted on the wings, strengthened with some of his most active musketeers and archers, who in agility and speed were almost as good as horsemen. Their duty was to prevent the enemy's horse from surrounding him, a task they accomplished gallantly beyond all expectation and belief. The right wing he assigned to James Hay and Nathaniel Gordon, the left to Sir William Rollock, all men of conspicuous courage. The left wing of the enemy was directed by Lewis Gordon son of the Marquess of Huntly, a bold, fiery, but fickle youth, who had forced his father's friends and clansmen, much to their distaste, to take up arms against Montrose.

The ground he occupied being a level plain suited to a cavalry engagement, he charged Montrose's right wing.

Observing the danger, Montrose sent Rollock with his twenty horse to their assistance. Ably supported by the courage of their officers and the activity of the picked footmen, they gave the enemy such a warm reception, that, though only forty-four to three hundred, they threw their ranks into disorder, and repulsed them with heavy loss. But being themselves so few, they did not dare to pursue them further. The great prudence of their officers on this occasion contributed largely to the victory; for the enemy now charged Montrose's left wing, exposed for want of the horse.

With admirable promptness he at once transferred his horse, after the rout of Lewis Gordon, to his left. As they were too few to show front to the enemy's more extended line, by a flank movement they avoided their first onset; then wheeling with great dexterity, they charged their flank, fell on them sword in hand, cut them down, and scattered them in flight. Forbes of Craigievar, a man of rank among the enemy, and Forbes of Boyndlie were taken prisoners. The rest they permitted to retreat in safety, as they were too few to venture on pursuit.

The leaders of the enemy's horse were more enraged by this second disgrace than dismayed by their loss; and imputing their defeat to the light musketeers who had been stationed among the horse, they sent for infantry from their own centre, intending to renew the fight with greater spirit. Montrose foresaw this, but was unwilling to expose this handful of brave men to a fresh attack, especially as their horses were spent with the two previous encounters, while the enemy were now reinforced by infantry. He had already observed that the enemy's horse were still in confusion and at a considerable distance from their foot. He therefore rode up to his own foot, who were exposed to a galling fire from the enemy's cannon, and addressed them as follows:

> We shall gain nothing, my men, by fighting at a distance. Who can distinguish the strong from the weak, the coward from the brave? Get to close quarters with yon craven feeble striplings; they will never withstand your valour. Fall on them with sword and musket-butts. Crush them; drive them off the field, and take vengeance on the traitor rebels.

Scarce had he given the word when they charged, and hurling them into confusion, put them to utter rout. Their horse also, who were waiting for the foot to help them, when they saw them flying, galloped off the field.

The victors, unable to pursue, much less to come up with them, let them escape in safety. But the foot they dealt with very differently, few of them escaping with their lives; for, as they had nowhere to fly to except the city, the victors and vanquished rushed in pell-mell through the gates and posterns, and the streets of the whole town were heaped with the slain.

Among others, an Irishman was observed trailing his leg, so shattered at the thigh by a cannon-ball that it hung by a mere shred of skin. Observing his comrades somewhat dismayed at his misfortune, he hailed them with a loud, cheery voice, 'Ha, Comrades, such is the luck of war; neither you nor I should be sorry for it. Do your work manfully. As for me, sure my Lord Marquess will make me a trooper, now I am no good for the foot.' With these words he coolly drew his knife, without flinching cut away the skin with his own hand, and gave the leg to a comrade to bury. Eventually he recovered of his wound and was actually made a trooper, in which service he afterwards showed great fidelity and courage. This battle was fought at Aberdeen on the 12th of September 1644. Montrose, having recalled his men to their colours, entered the city and allowed them two days.

Auldearn

Wishart's account of the fight of Auldearn causes the greatest debate and controversy. The battle, a confused brawl, in which the Royalists were very nearly defeated by Montrose's failure to set up a proper screen of piquets, is portrayed by Wishart as a victory worthy of Caeser for the Marquess. In reality it was a victory snatched from the jaws of defeat by MacColla and the veteran cavalry of Lord Gordon.

Next day, Montrose encamped at the village of Auldearn. Hurry, as he had expected, found the Earls of Seaforth and Sutherland, the Clan Eraser, with most of the men of Moray, Caithness and the neighbourhood, assembled in arms at Inverness.

With these and the veterans of the town garrison he marched straight for Montrose. The force under his command numbered 3,500 foot and 400 horse. Montrose, who had not more than 1,500 foot and 250 horse, was now very anxious to retire. But Hurry pressed him so hard that retreat was almost out of the question. Moreover, Baillie with the southern army, which was still more formidable in cavalry, had already crossed the Grampians, and was now far on his way to the Spey, marching in great haste. What was to be done? Either Montrose must fight with Hurry, or take the far more serious risk of being hemmed in between the gathering forces of the enemy. He therefore resolved to risk a battle at once, leaving the issue to Providence, and chose an advantageous position to await the enemy. The village stood on a low ridge and covered a neighbouring hollow.

Behind it are some hillocks, which conceal it from the view of all but those who are close upon it. In the hollow he drew up his forces, which were quite invisible to the enemy. In front of the village he stationed a few picked foot-soldiers, men of experience and prompt to act, along with his cannon, masked by some dykes which had been cast up there. The right wing he entrusted to Alastair Macdonald with 400 foot, stationed on ground which happened to be defended by dykes and ditches, brushwood and rocks. These he ordered to reserve themselves, whatever happened, and not to quit their position, which formed a strong natural fortification, secure from any attack either of horse or of foot. To this division was consigned the well-known royal standard, broadly displayed, which used to be carried only before Montrose,—an admirable ruse, calculated to draw the main attack upon that impregnable position, so as to give him an opportunity for a successful attack upon the left. With this object he transferred all the rest of his men to the opposite wing, himself taking command of the foot, and Lord Gordon in charge of the horse. His main centre was left to the imagination of the enemy. In fact, he had none, but a small body stationed under cover of the dykes before the village made a show of one. With so small a force a reserve was out of the question.

As Montrose by this skilful arrangement had foreseen, the enemy no sooner observed the royal standard, than they sent the best part of their horse, with the veterans who formed their main strength, against that point, and commenced the assault upon the right wing and those who were posted before the village, keeping up a determined attack by constant relays of fresh men. This Montrose, with so few men, could not do. He therefore resolved to charge at once with the whole weight of his left. Just as he was on the point of giving effect to this resolution, a messenger, on whose fidelity and prudence he could rely, whispered in his ear, 'Macdonald and his right wing are routed.'

To prevent a panic among his men at the bad news, with admirable presence of mind he at once called out:

Come, my Lord Gordon, what are we waiting for? Our friend Macdonald on the right has routed the enemy and is slaughtering the fugitives. Shall we look on idly and let him carry off all the honours of the day?

With these words he hurled his line upon the enemy. The shock of the Gordons was irresistible. After a brief struggle, Hurry's horse wavered, recoiled, wheeled, and fled, leaving their own flanks naked and exposed. Though deserted by the horse, the infantry, being superior in numbers and much better armed, stood their ground bravely, until Montrose came to close quarters, and forced them to fling down their arms and make a desperate but vain attempt to save themselves by flight. Montrose, however, did not forget the news his trusty messenger had brought. Followed by some of his promptest men, he wheeled to the right, where he found matters in a very different condition. Macdonald, a brave man, but readier with his hand than his head, hasty in battle and bold to rashness, stung by the taunts and scoffs of the enemy, disdained to shelter himself behind dykes and bushes, and, contrary to orders, threw himself with his men outside of their strong position. His rashness cost him dear.

The enemy, who were far stronger both in horse and numbers, and most of them veteran troops, drove his men back pell-mell, and had he not withdrawn them to a neighbouring enclosure just in time, they would every one of them have been lost, and the royal standard with them. Rash as he had been, he atoned for his error by his splendid courage in bringing off his men. The last to retire, and covering himself with a huge target, single-handed he withstood the thickest of the enemy. Some of the pikemen, by whom he was hard pressed, again and again pierced his target with the points of their weapons, which he mowed off with his broadsword by threes and fours at a sweep. But when those who were assailing the enclosure saw Montrose coming to the rescue, and their own men on the left put to rout, the horse fled headlong, but the foot, mostly veterans from Ireland, fought on doggedly, and fell man by man almost where they stood. The victors followed the fugitives for some miles. Of the enemy there fell about 3,000 foot, of whom the veterans had fought with conspicuous bravery. Most of the cavalry escaped by a flight more timely than honourable. Even Hurry himself, with some of his best men, who were the last to quit the field, would not have escaped, had not the Viscount Aboyne carelessly displayed some ensigns and standards which he had captured in the rout, and instead of pursuing the fugitives turned to his own men, who took him for a fresh force coming on to renew the attack. The mistake lasted long enough to give the enemy's horse, though broken, time to scatter and fly by such paths as they happened to know or hit on. A few of them made their way with Hurry to Inverness before next morning.

The most distinguished of the enemy who fell were Campbell of Lawers, colonel of one of the old regiments, Sir John Murray, Sir Gideon Murray, and some other brave men, whose loss might have been deplored, had they not stained their valour by the infamous crime of rebellion. In this they had not followed their own judgment, but the impulse of the mob or the ambition and avarice of their chiefs. Of those who fought with Montrose on the left, he lost one only, a private soldier. On the other wing, where Macdonald commanded, he lost fourteen, also common soldiers, but a very large number were wounded. Montrose himself took care that these should be safely housed and receive medical attention. As for the prisoners, he consoled them with courtesy and gentleness. Those who repented of their rebellion he set at liberty or enlisted in his own service. The stubborn he lodged in various prisons.

II – Patrick Gordon of Ruthven's account of the battles of Inverlochy, Auldearn and Kilsyth from *A Short Abridgement of Britane's Distemper*

Patrick Gordon was born in 1606, the son of Thomas Gordon of Cluny and Elizabeth Douglas, and was a kinsman to Lewis Gordon, 3rd Marquess of Huntly. He naturally wrote from a Gordon perspective and as such he is a necessary counterbalance to Wishart's very pro-Montrose narratives.

Inverlochy

Gordon describes Montrose's veteran Irish regiments using the European/ Swedish salvo method to disorder and rout their opponents.

> He commanded by the major not to giue fyre till he gaue it in there breastes, and this course in the right wing he rightly obserues also; and thus patiently receaueing there shote, without giueing fyre, till they fyred there beardes, both winges make a cruell hauoke of the enemies; leapeing in amongst them with there swordes and targates, they quickly put them to disorder, and disperses them ower all the fieldes.
>
> Wpon Sonday, the second of Februarie, being Candlemasse day, anno 1645, about the sune rysseing, both the armies drawes wp in battell. By Auchinbreike, as generall for that day, the two regimentes Argyll had brought from Sterling ware placed in the right and leaft winges, and some highlanders with them; there wan was a strong battaillon of highlanderes, with gunes, bowes, and axes; in the reire or maine battail, ware all there pryme men, and the greatest strenth of the armie, with two peice of ordinance.
>
> The marquisse of Montrose diuides his armie also in foure battelles, the major, Alexander M'Donald, had the leading of the right winge; colonell Occaen had the leading of the leaft wing, both those ware Irishes; the Stewartes of Apine, with those of Atholle, Glenco, and Lochaber, had the wane. Donald Farquharsone was gone to raise more forces in Banzenoch and the rest, of Huntlyes highlandes. M'Collein, the captane of the clane Randell, and Glengerrie had the reire brought wp by collonell James M'Coneil. The marquise had a reserue of Irishes and other highlanders. It fell Occaen, with the leaft wing, to charge Ardgylles right wing; he commanded by the major not to giue fyre till he gaue it in there breastes, and this course in the right wing he rightly obserues also; and thus patiently receaueing there shote, without giueing fyre, till they fyred there beardes, both winges make a cruell hauoke of the enemies; leapeing in amongst them with there swordes and targates, they quickly put them to disorder, and disperses them ower all the fieldes. There wan, by this, perceauing themselfes naked, and there winges brockin and dispersed that should flanked them, did hardly withstand the shoke of Montrose wan, who charged them, and followed there charge in a close bodie, with such strenth and furie as they ware forced to giue backe wpon there reire; who, instead of opineing there rankes to receaue them, and giue the enemies a new charge, they queit there standing, brakes there ordour, and flies confusedly towardes the castell, wheirin they had pleaced fyftie souldiours. Sir Thomas Ogiluie, with a troupe of horse, afrontes tuo hundreth of them that made for the castell, and forced them to flie with the rest wp the syd of the laike or firth. In this conflick,

this brawe gentleman receaued a shote, whereof he died soonne after, to the no small regrait of the whole armie.

The marquisse of Ardgyll, standing of a litle in the sea, and had seene this ouerthrow, to his great griefe no doubt, not stayeing to see his enemies persewe the flight, which continowed for seauin or eight mylles; and if they had not beene wyried with a long mairch, standeing all the night after in battell, and fanteing for want of food, there had few or non eschaped. In this battell, the laird of Auchinbreeke was killed, with fourteine barrones of the name of Cambell, tuo and tuantie men of qualitie taken prisoneres, and seauinteine hundreth killed of the armie.

In the castell of Inverlochie there ware fyftie of the Sterling regiment, with there commanderes, that got there lyues; but of tuo hunder highlanders, none eschaped the clane Donald furie. This happie and fortunat leader, haueing set all thinges in order after the battell, retyres towardes Murrav with his small but wictorious armie.

Auldearn

Gordon's account of the battle is somewhat more objective than Wishart's. He is critical of the failure of the Royalists to deploy scouts, and supportive of the actions of both Alasdair MacColla and Lord Gordon, whose intervention with cavalry help turn the tide of victory.

When they began ther marche, the rain began also, and conteinued the wholl night. Wherefor when they wer com within four myles they halt, and advysed what shall be don with ther muskets, which they wer perswadded the rain had poysoned. To draw the charge would spend too much tym; wherefor they resolued to turne down to the eeasyd, and ther diaeharpp them, being then fyve myles from ther enemie, and therefor confident that the report of a musket coutd not be so far hard. They wer confident alsu that the waters, as they wsuallie do, would carrie the sound from the land.

But the thundering report of this vollie, contrairie to ther expectation, was, by a suddain changeing of the wynd, carried throw the aire wnlo the eares of fyve or six scouts, whom the major before day had send forth, as God would have it, and those gave quickly intelligence and alarum to the campe, and certified the major; who, for all his dilligence, could hardly get two regiments drawen up, on of the Irishes, and on of Huntlie, when the enemie wer com in sight, this wnlookt for charge bred such confusion in the campe.

The major, with those two regiments, advanceth a little befor the town, towards a marishe and som bushes, which was a stronge ground, and fencible against horsmen, wher it fell him to receive the first charge of the euemie, whill Montros gathered the rest of the foot; and having the town and som little biles betuxt bim and the enemie, drawes them wpe. My lord Gordon and his brother quickly got the horsmen together, appoynting the best men, and sucbe as they knew wold not leave them, to attend ther owne personcs. Caimburrow being on whom my lord appoynted nixt his person, whom he knew to be faithful! and trustie, as, besyds his currage, he knew his wpright heart and intier love would never suffer him to leave him. Arradoull was appoynted by Aboyne to attend nixt to his person.

Whill Montros drawes wp the foot to oppose the maine body of the enemies hattell, Ahoyn drawes a hundreth horse to charge the right winge, and my lord Gordon drawes forth ao many to charge the left winge; whill M'Donell, who led the vane of the armie, is charged wilh a stronge regiment of foot, and two troopes of horse. So, efter a brave and long maintained resistance, he is forced a reteir to som yeards of the town, and from thence to keipe them of wilh conteinuall shot, which a little quealed ther force, and advanceth the aecund tym, and with great currage and extreum vallour charges them; but the ground wpon bis left hand being all quagmyre and bushes, was in this sccund charge extreamly to bis dissadvantage, wher his men could nether advance in order, nor fynd sure footting to stand, nor marche forward to helpe ther fellowes.

The enemie, coming wp two regiments in a full body, flanked with horsemen, did charge the major in that deficult place; and the rest of ther maine battell following. One regiment still seconding ane other; yet efter a stronge and obsteinat resistance, he manteines his station with invinceible curage a long tym, till, opprest with multitude, and charge wpon charge, he was forced to give ground, and with great deficuly, befor he could reteir his people in good order, or keipe them from confuised fieight; and altho he was forced to quyt his ground, yet this brave and valorous gentlman keipt his secund retreat still in a pouster of defence. He was ever in the frount, and his strenth, his curage, and dexterittie let his enemies sie, even with terror, wonderfull feats of armes for his fellowcs to imitate, his strong arme cutting asunder whatsoever or whosoever did him resist. He brack two swords; and when they had fastened a number of pickes in his tairge, wherwith they could have born down thre or four ordinarie men to the ground, they could not mak him to shirink, or bow so much as on kne to the ground; but with on blow of his sword the strenth of his vallorous arme cute all the picks asunder that stuck in his target, whill non durst approach within the lenth of his weappon. When he had don what was possible, or rather what was wnpossible to be don by any other but himselfe, so great wer the numberes of trained men who did charge and weell neir inviron those two regiments which he led, the horsmen being wnable to assault him for the dycks of the yeards which he keipt for his retreit, but almost the wholl body of the foot readdy to incompass him, then for griefe was he ready to burst, seing non to secund him, and saw no hope of victorie, but all the simptoms of a disastrous and dreadful overthrow. Wherefor he called to those that werabout him, 'Ach, meseoures,' said he, 'sail our enemies by this on dayes work be able to wreast out of our hands all the glorie that we have formerly gained. Let it never be said that a basse flight shall bear witnes of it, or that our actiones should seam to confesse so much; but let ws die bravely; let it never be thought that they have triumphed over our currage, nor the loayltie we ow to our soveraigne lord, and let ws hope the best. God is stronge eneugh.

And whill he whispered those words, for he would not speak aloud, least the enemies might imagine of yeilding, behold how gratious Heavin and the Devyn Power did assist him.

My lord of Aboyn, that had gotten ane hundreth brave gentelmen about him, perseveing the danger, and weell forseing that the discomfitore of the infantre was the overthrow of the wholl armie, resolves, by a violent charge, to change the fortoun of the day, or die by the way. Wherfor he fales in vpon the right winge, for from thence cam the greatest danger, and they receive his charge with auch a conteinuall giveing of fyre, as he aemed, by the thick smok throw which he went, to asalt a terrible cloud of thunder and lightening; but his charge was so brave and resolved, as if it had bein a devowreing or swellowing gulfe, he had aitber smothered it by going throw it, or atopt it by leiping in; as did that famous man who atopt the gulf at Room, by leiping horse and man unto it; for he with that small body of horse, who stood to their lord and leidder as if they had bein but on man, did, with ane violent fortitude, overcom all resistance, and beats them out of order so soundly, that the best advysed amongst them knew not wheron to resolve; so furrious was the charge, so weell followed, and so constantly manteind, as he did not only breck and disperse them, but such as strove to keipe themselves togither, as if they intended to ralley and mak head again. Thus, with a new charge, he did still crushe in peices, following the task he had begun with such ane earnest desyre to overcom, as whersoever he cam, they wer beatten down befor him, so weell was he followed, and so closley did those gallent gentlemen stick to him; and when he followed those that fled till ther was non left to resist him, he returned to sie what mor was to be don, his followeres, loaded with cullores taken from ther vanquished enemies; and those cullors being four or fjve, wer evident witnesse that this on troope had beat so many troopes of the enemies.

And it is said that the major cryed out when he saw this charge, so tymlie intended, and so bravely followed forth; 'Now,' said he, 'those ar indeid the vallient Gordoues, and worthie of that name which fame hath caried abroad of them.'

The main battell of the Covenant stood inteir all this tym, and haveing twyse gained ground and forced the Royalists to reteir, whom M'Donell had always keipt in order, they hopt to have made it a certain victorie; but now ther right wing being thus wholly defate, and seeing the danger from thence of a new charge, without hope of being secunded, they began to fear the event, wnles ther horsmen in the left wing could clear the field befor them.

The marques of Montrose having at lenth gotten the body of the foot togither, advances wp to M'Donell, to mak on body against the strenth of ther enemies, who could have incompassed them if it had bein in a large plain feild. My lord Gordon by this time charges the left winge, and that with a new form of fight, for he discharges all shootting of pistoles and carrabines, only with ther swords to charge quyt throwgh ther enemies, who wer so many in number, and so stronge and weell horsed, as if by a desperat charge they got them not broken, it was too apparrent that they might recover the day. But Aboyn having overthrowen the right winge, and the main battell left bair on that syd, and seeing Montrose and M'Donell joyned to give a new charge, the great body began to stagger, all their hopes being in ther left winge; and that my lord Gordon charges so soundly, with swords only, as if they scorned to be resisted; they had all sworn to go throw or dye. Nor did they stay heir, but having broken the horsemen and sett them to run for ther lyfe, then wheeling about wher Lawers with the thre trained regiments stood, nor knew they what it was to turne ther back, nor could they be broken till now that my lord Gordon pressed through them; and then you should have sein how the infantrie of the Royalists, keiping togither and following the charge of the horsmen, did tear and cut them in peices, even in rankes and fyles, as they stood, so great was the execution which they made efter the horse had shanken and quyt astonished them, by perseing rudly throw them, as it was very lamentable to behold ... of the great slaughter; for ther lay tuantie eight hundreth, many sayes three thousand, dead one the place; and of the Royalistes saxteine, whereof there was fourteine of McDonald's regiement, who had borne the first bout and sorresi of the day. This battell was foghten the Bynth of May, on a Fryday, in iheyeere 1645."

Kilsyth

Whereas Wishart and others give the credit of victory to the Highland contingent in Montrose's army, Gordon identifies the Royalist superiority in numbers of cavalry as the crucial factor. This statement was supported by William Baillie, commander of the opposing forces. The Royalist Horse, like its Covenant counterpart, would have been very much at home on the battlefields of England and further afield in Europe, equipped as they were for the main as modern European harquebusiers.

A strong partie from the estates armie was send before to ingadge the Royalists; and this partie consisted of three regiments, that of the reide cottes, and other tuo, in the midte whereof ware placed tuo troupes of horse, and one of lanciers to flanke them.

The horse troupes adwanceth befor the foot to gaine a high ground; hut was sharply encountered by adjutant Gordoune, who was send befor the armie to gaine that same high ground, and charged them so soundly as he beat them backe againe within the bodie of ther foote; and, followeing his charge with too much wnadwissed courage, was in euident danger to be lossed, for the armie yet had not begune to adwance, being not fullie in ordour of battell. Those thre regimentes, without brakeing of there ordour, lets them enter amongst them, and glueing fyre on all sydes, had well neire encompassed them: wheirwpon McAleine, with his regiment, and Glengerrie with his, who had taken ane higher ground, there being no more of the foot as yet adwanced, and stood at so lairge a distance as they could giue no aide to the adjutant thus ingadged, they cryed out that, if the horsemen adwanced not more speedily, the losse of those troupes would indanger the whole armie.

Aboyne haueing taken with him his tualfe gentlemen to attend him, and heareing how the hylanderes cryed for the horsemen's more speedie adwancement, and coming forward to see the danger, he perceaues the adjutant ingadged and ouer partied, by reason of which he and all that was with him should be aither cute in peices, if they stood out, or if they for refuge fled back to the main body, they might raise a powwant with such confusion as might undoubtedly hazard the losse of that day. Where-for, being mightily discontented with the adjutant raish ingadgement, he postes one backe to cause the horsemen adwance speedily, if the whole armie ware not as yet readie; and to show colonel Gordoune that himselfe was ingadged, and therefor desyred the marquisse to make haist. When he send this commission backe, his noble heart could not indure to see his lerwantes and kinsmen stand so brawely too it, and yet so ouer maistered with power, as if they ware not secunded they ware all lost. Wherefor he cryes to those fewe that followed him, 'Let ws goe, monseours, and assist these our distressed freindes, in so great hazart throw the foolish raishenes of there commander. We shall, God willing, bring them of, at least in some good order, so as they shall nether be all lost, nor indanger the armie by there suddaine flight, whereto they may be forced.' And thus he who in all his resolutiones was dexterous, prompte, and readie, not stayeing for answer, least they sould striue to detaine him from so dangerous a taske with so small a number, he putes his horse to the gallope, and so tyed them to follow. He charged wpon the lanciers, who flanked the reid regiment; and they seing him so furiously to come wpon them, retyres to the leaft hand, puteing the foot betwixt them and him. He, without atayeing, charges forward wpon the foote, till, being come within pistol-shote, he perceaues them fitte there pickes, for the front ware all pickemen. Wherefor, with admirable desleritie, and a nimble resolution, he raines his horee a lilte to the leift hand, and charges with such resolution and baist wpon the flanke of the reid regiment, which ware all muscatyres, that, altho they gaue him three volies of shotte from the three 6rat rankes, yet he charged quyt throw them, till be came where bis distreaaed freinds ware inuironed both with horse and foote, whose ordour they could not gett broke; but being charged one all hands, was euin to call for quarterea, or desperatly to bracke throw thera, and flie backe to there armie: but bis comeing in good tyme makes them rely, and quickly to joine with bis followers, to whom he cryed, 'Courrage, my heartes; follow me, and let tbem haue one sound charge.' And this he gives with such braue and invincible resolution, as he brackes, disperses, and discourages both foote and horse, who seekes no more to persewe, but stryues to retyre in order, to the which there commanderea often invites them, but in waine. They were once with Aboyne bis braue charge at first, and now with a stronger second charge, so broken and diejoyned, that they begane to run for there lyues, while the constant and noble earle of Airely is, by the generallea appoyntraent, adwanceingi for when Aboyne's messenger came assureing the gernrll that, to relioue the adjutant, Aboyne was ingadged, this inflamed so the currage of the horse-men, as they could hardly he keipt in order, but would have rune headlonges to the releefe of there lord, there cheife, and there commander. Yet Airely adwances with his braue troupe of Ogilvies, all of his own kine and followers: colonell Gordone is ordained to follow and second him with the whole bodie of horse; and altbo noble Airly comes wp in so good tyme, as he makes sure worke of that which Aboyne hud luiccalie begune, brakeing the other tua regimentes which had stand intyre without chargeing or being charged till now, with there horse troupes in such manner, that they stood aa if they had intended to make some resistence, but now glueing themselves for wanquissed, throweing doune there armes, and runneing for there lyues. By this tyrac was colonell Gordoune come vp with ane intyre body of foure hunder horae, ao aa the whole three regimentes, with there troupes, were io wiolently beat backe wpon the bodie of there armie, not yet brought vp in order, that they are all put to coofueioa, and so, without resolution, voto ane wntymely flight.

III – Lieutenant-General William Baillie's Accounts[2]

By way of comparison, the account of Lieutenant-General William Baillie, the officer in charge of the government forces account is included here. Baillie was seemingly driven to distraction by the constant interference by the Government committee that was attached to his command: 'I found myself so slighted in every thing belonging to ane commander-in-chieffe,

---

2. Taken from Baillie, Robert, *Letters and Journals* (Edinburgh, 1842).

that for the short time I wes to stay with them, I would absolutely submitt to their direction, and follow it'.

First paper

My Lords And Gentlemen, In obedience to your command, whereby I wes required to informe yow of the conduct of your forces since my dimission at Perth, untill that unhappie day at Killsyth, your Lordships shall be pleased to know, that at the acceptance of my dimission, the Honourable House of Parliament desyred me to attend their forces untill the coming of these appointed to succeed unto me; whilk I indeavoured to vaesse, and that because I being so highlie scandalized, while I had charge, and served the Estate by commission; if then, serving as it were at discretion, any thing should miscarrie, or fall out amisse, undoubtedlie the aspersions of the malitious, and my sufferings would be doubled. This proved not satisfactorie; and therefore, yielding unto their pressings, I wes content to wait upon their service a fourtnight; in which tyme, such as they had appointed for the charge, as I imagined, might both be advertised, and repaire unto them, if diligence had been used. Immediatelie thereafter the rebells returned from the hills into Logyalmond; and I, with consent of the Lords and others of the Committee who were then present, marched to the south side of the Bridge of Earne, hopefull the regiments of Fyfe should have joyned with us there. Upon the second day thereafter the rebells, having crossed Earne at or about Dinning, presented themselves before our quarter, whilk, with consent of these were of the Committee, I had caused fortifie alse weel as tyme would suffer, for which the rebells marched up towards the hisis on the right hand. Upon the morrow, the rebells marched into the [Mills] of Forth; and I, by advyce of the Committee, brought their forces that night to Lindores, and on the morrow to the hill above Rossie; where the regiments of Fyfe, for whom the Earle of Crawfurd had ridden to Coupar the night before, did joyne with us. That night, with advyce of these of the Committee, we lodged near unto Burghlie. The next day, by their advyce, I marched and lodged that night betwixt Sauchie and the bridge of Tullibody. Upon the morrow, hearing the rebells had crossed Forth above Stirling, these of the Committee then present, advysed we should crosse at Stirling; and a little above the parke, upon the southwest side thereof, I halted with the five regiments, untill these of Fyfe were brought up, hearing the rebells were marched toward Kilsyth. After the upcoming of these regiments, the Marquess of Argyle, Earle of Crawfurd, and Lord Burghlie, and with them, if I mistake not, the Earle of Tullibardin, the Lords Elcho and Balcarras, with some others, came up. My Lord Marquess asked me, What wes next to be done? I answered, The direction should come from his Lordship, and these of the Committee. My Lord demanded what reason wes for that? I answered, I found myself so slighted in every thing belonging to ane commander-in-chieffe, that for the short time I wes to stay with them, 1 would absolutely submit to their direction, and follow it. The Marquess desired me to explain myself, which I did in three particulars, sufficiently known to my Lord Marquess, and the other Lords and gentlemen then present. I told his Lordship, Prisoners of all sorts were exchanged without my knowledge: the traffickers therein receaved passes from others; and sometymes passing within two myles of me, did neither acquaint me with their business, nor, at their returne, where, or in what posture they had left the enemie. Secondlie, While I wes present, others did sometymes undertake the command of the armie. Thirdly, Without either my order or knowledge, fyre wes raised, and that destroyed which might have been ane recompence to some good deserver; for which I could not be answerable to the publique. Which considered, I should in every thing freely give my owne opinion, but follow the judgement of the Committee, and the rather because that wes the last day of my undertaking. From that our march to the bridge of Denny wes agreed upon, and from that to the Hollin-buss, where we lodged that night, some two myles and ane halfe from Killsyth; where the rebells quartered likewise. On the next morning, the Marquess came to the head of our quarter, accompanied with the Lord Burghlie, or some other, whom of I doe not weell remember: his Lordship enquired of the rebells, who, I told him, were still att Killsyth. His Lordship asked, If we might not advance nearer them? I answered, we were near enough if we intended not to sight, and that his Lordship knew weell enough how rough and uneasie a way that was to march in. My Lord replyed, we needed not keep the hie-way, bot march over at nearest. I desyred the Earle of Crawfurd and others might be called, who were in the next tent; who, when they come, consented to our advanceing, and I marched with the regiments through the corns and over the braes, untill the unpaisible ground did hold us up. There I imbattelled, where I doubt, if on any quarter twenty men on front could either have gone from us or attack us. At the upcoming of the noblemen and others of the Committee, whom I doe not so weell remember, it wes asked me by the Lords, but by whom in particular I have forgott, If we could not draw up to the hill on our right hand? I shew them I did not conceave that ground to be good, and that the rebells (if they would) might possess themselves of it before us. Their Lordships then desired that some might be sent to visite the ground; which was done. In the mean time, I went with my Lord Elcho and my Lord Burghlie to the right hand of the regiments. Not long after, I wes sent for by the other noblemen, and I desired the Lord Elcho and Burghlie to goe with me, conjectureing they would press our removeing; which at our coming they did, alleadging the advantage might be had of the enemies from that field, they being, as they supposed, allready upon their march westward. I liked not the motion: I told them, if the rebells should seek to ingadge us there, I conceaved they should have great advantage of us; farder, if we should beat them to the hill, it would be unto us no great advantage: But, as I had said, upon like disputes near unto Methven and the Bridge of Earne, to us the loss of the day would be the loss of the kingdome. This was not satisfactorie; and therefore I gathered the voices of such of the Committee as were there, namely, the Marquess Argyle, the Earles of Crawfurd and Tullibardine, the Lords Elcho, Burghlie, and Balcarras; who the rest were, I remember not; but all agreed to draw unto the hill except Balcarras. This resolution wes immediately followed. The commanded men, with the horsemen, marched before; the regiment on the right hand, faceing to the right hand, and so the rest advanced to the hill; where, I suppose, that wes done by me which wes incumbent unto me in all that the shortness of time would suffer before we were engaged. Whereof, and of what wes done without or against order, your Honours may be pleased to consider, by the sigure in this other paper. If I wes either the last in the sight, or the first in the flight, I leave to the testimony of the Marquess's officers and Colonell Hume's, and unto Generall-Major Hollburne; with whom, after these three regiments were broken, I came off on the reare of these horses of the rebells who broke the Earle of Crawfurd. Thus your Lordships have, to my best remembrance, what yow did require of me, wherby I hope it shall be evident, that I did nothing of consequence at no time, bot either with the assent or advyce of these members of the Committee of State, whose advice I wes obliedged to take, and who had power to call me to ane accompt for my actions, as likewise to governe the army, whilk they did practise and make use of, even while by commission I wes in charge. How dangerous then, (I pray your Honours to consider,) had it been for me, being without commission, to have slighted their advyce and counsell, yea, even though no prejudice should have followed thereupon?

Second paper

My Lords And Gentlemen, Being appointed by your Honours, at your last meeting, that I should enlarge my relation concerning the advanceing and ingadgeing with the rebells near unto Killsyth, in all the circumstances and passages thereof, and of every man's particular behaviour thereintill, in so farr as I could remember; yow shall be pleased to know, that in my former paper, I shew your Honors, that conforme to the resolution of these of the Committee, who were present, I sent the commanded musqueteers to the hill, and desired Major Halden to be their guide unto ane inclosure which I pointed out unto him; he did it. I followed them immediately with my Lord Balcarras and the horsemen, giving order to the foot to follow us, as I mentioned in my first paper. I desyred my Lord Balcarras, that the horsemen might stay near unto the commandit musqueteers; which wes done. I advanced my selse where there stood a number of gentlemen on horseback, where I found five ratt musqueteers, more than ane musquet-shott at randome before their bodie, without any order from me. The Earle Crawfurd, my Lord Burghlie, and I, galloped over the brae to see the posture of the enemie, who were embattelled in the meadow, and sundries of them disbanded, were falling up the glen through the bushes. At our returne to thebraehead, we fand the Marquess of Argyle, with sundry others, and we saw Major Halden leading up an partie of musqueteers over the field, and toward a house near the glen, without any order from me; neither did they come off when I sent Colonell Arnot, and thereafter Rootmaster Blair, to Major Halden, for that purpose: wherefore seeing the rebells fall up strong, I desired them to reteire, and the officers to goe to their charge. My Lord Balcarras and I galloped back to the regiments. He asked me what he should doe? I desired him to draw up his regiment on the right hand of the Earle Lauderdale's. I gave order to Lauderdale's, both by myselfe and my adjutant, to face to the right hand, and to march to the foot of the hill, then to face as they were; to Hume to follow their stepps, halt when they halted, and keep distance and front with them. The Marquess his Major, as I went toward him, asked what he should doe? I told him, he should draw up on Hume's left hand, as he had done before. I had not ridden farr from him, when looking back, I find Hume had left the way I had put him in, and wes gone at a trott, right west, in among the dykes and toward the enemy. I followed alse fast as I could ryde, and meeting the Adjutant on the way, desired him he should bring up the Earle Crawfurd's regiment to Lauderdale's left hand, and cause the Generall-Major Leslie draw up the regiments of Fyfe in reserve as of before: but before I could come to Hume, he and the other two regiments, to wit, the Marquess of Argyle's, and the three that were joyned in one, had taken in ane inclosure, from whilk (the enemy being so near) it wes impossible to bring them off. I rode down on the reere, and returned on their front. The rebells foot, be this tyme, were approached to the next dyke, on whom our musqueteers made more fire than I could have wished; and therefore did I what I could, with the assistance of such of the officers as were known unto me, to make them spare their shott till the enemy should be at an nearer distance, and to keep up the musqueteers with their picks and collors; but to no great purpose. In end, the rebells leapt over the dyke, and with downe heads fell on and broke these regiments. The present officers whom I remember, were Hume, his Lieutenant-Collonell and major of the Marquess's regiment, Lieutenant-Colonel Campbell, and Major Menzies, Glencairne's sergeant-major, and Cassills's Lieutenant-Collonell, with sundry others, who behaved themselves weell, and whom of I saw none carefull to save themselves before the routing of the regiments. Thereafter I rode to the brae, where I found Generall-Major Hollburne alone, who shew me a squadron of the rebells horsemen, who had gone by and charged the horsemen with Lieutenant-Collonell Murray, and, as I supposed, did afterward rowt the Earle of Crawfurd, and these with him; Hollburne and I galloped through the inclosures to have found the reserve; bot before we could come at them, they were in the flight. At the brook, that not long before we had crossed, we overtook Major Inglish of Inglistoune, Captain Maitland, and some other officers of the Fyfe regiments, who with me indeavoured to make our people stand, and maintaine that passe; bot all in vaine. Thereafter we rode off together till we past the Bridge of Denny; where we parted, and Hollburne and I went to Stirling, where, in presence of the Earle Tullibardine and the Lord Burghlie, I dealt with the horsemen that were there, to have gone with me to Clidsdale; but lost my labour; for they finding the bridge shut, crossed the river at the foord of Dripp, except the officers, who thereafter went in with us into the towne; where, by advyce of the Earle of Crawfurd, the other Lords and gentlemen that were there, the best course wes taken that might be for that tyme, for secureing that towne and castell.

It is objected against me only, as if no other officer were to give an accompt, neither for regiment, company, nor corporalship, that on this our unhappie day there were no lighted lunts among the musquetrie? The fire given by the first five regiments will sufficiently answer what concerns them; and for the other three, I humbly intreat your Honours to inform yourselves of Generall-Major Leslie, the Adjutant, and the chief officers of these severall regiments: if they doe not satiffie yow therein, then I shall answer for myselfe. Secondly, it is alleadged we should have marched from the one ground to the other in battell: which wes impossible, in regard of the ground, and our large front; neither could we have marched with single regiments, embattelled from the north fide of the water to the hill, but by turning ane narrow flanke of sex deep unto the enemy, against common sense, and in doing thereof, that same tyme that should have been lost drawing up upon the hill in the ground designed unto them, should lykwise have been lost, or rather more, at their imbattelling upon the waterside. Besides, they should have been obliedged to have wheeled once to the right hand, and when they had come into the ground, againe to the left hand, which had been a motion of great difficultie in that rough and unequall ground; wherefore my order wes, (as I esteem it,) absolutely the best, if it have your Honours approbation, that our battell which fronted to the enemy, and wes to march off to the right hand, should by the severall regiments face to the right hand, making the flanck the front; so that even upon our march, the faceing again to the left hand should have put us in our former posture and battell, if the enemy had attacked us on that way. Thirdly, It is said, I did neither give word nor signe. Whereunto I answer, At our first imbattelling it wes not yet tyme; then we saw no enemy but the outer guard, neither wes it resolved to sight, bot most men thought the rebells were marching west. After we left our ground, we had not tyme to imbattell compleatlie; which Souldattis thinks necessarie to be done before the giving of word or signe, neither had it been possible to have given them unto all the regiments in ane poynt of time. Farder, it cannot be alleadged, that the want of them made us losse the day, or that by the enemies signe we could not be knowne one from another. No ; the want of poynts of formalitie wes not the cause of the misfortouns of that day ; bot God, for our other sinns, did suffer us to fall before our enemies, whereof the only meane and occasion is only probable to have been our removeing from that ground whereon we stood first imbattelled, being soe near ane enemie who had sundrie advantages of us.

So by this and my former paper, your Honours may judge of my walking in your service since my dimission ; and if there be yet any that desires ane accompt of the disposition of things, and the many misfortouns of the countrey, whille I wes in charge, I shall not shelter myselfe with that approbation given at Stirling and Perth, bot shall endeavour to satisfie your desire, by deducing unto yow of new, and in particular, how little I wes enabled for performing so great service as wes required of me, and let yow see my care to have preserved your forces when little could have been atcheived with them, in regard both of their numbers, of the season, and of the places where the enemy wes to be found; and, last of all, I am confident your Honors shall perceave, that the losses at Innerlochie, Aldearne, and Alfoord, were not procured neither through my negligence nor counsel.

Colour Plate Commentaries

Plate A
1. Irish Ensign.
As was typical of Irish regimental colours in Scotland in the 'year of miracles' this ensign's flag features the cypher 'Vivat Carolus Rex' under a red saltire on a yellow canton. The yellow field and the overt Catholic imagery dominating the main field of the flag are sourced from two contemporary flag descriptions as preserved by the Irish Franciscan Fr Luke Wadding. The motto below reads 'Aequum est pro Christo mori' (It is fitting to die for Christ). This ensign is not particularly well dressed so it may be surmised that this impression is representative of early on in the campaign prior to the seizure of supplies in terms of accoutrements and clothing in Aberdeen or Perth. His close fitting trews are in a diagonal plaid weave as was common in Ireland as well as the Scottish Highlands at the time as evidenced by archaeological finds in Killery (Co Sligo) and Dungiven (Co Derry). (Photo: Dave Swift/Interpreter: Sebastian Stock © Claíomh 2014)

2. MacColla Lifeguard.
Highlander in 'belted plaid' or fíle mór and 'double armed' with both bow and matchlock musket as seen in a depiction of an 'Irishman' in the Swedish service in a 1631 German broadsheet. The basket hilted sword was now the ubiquitous Scots Highland melée weapon of choice as the old double handed 'twahondit' sword had declined in use since the dawn of the century. The doublet is based on a bog find from Dungiven in Co Derry. (Photo: Niamh O'Rourke/Interpreter: Dave Swift © Claíomh 2014)

Plate B
1. Irish Musketeer.
At the core of Montrose' army were his regular troops. A significant portion of these regular forces were made up of a brigade of Irish infantry. In September 1643 a ceasefire to the conflict in Ireland was organised by the King's representative, the Marquis of Ormonde. This would enable extra troops to be used in England and Scotland. In February 1644 the Irish Confederate Supreme Council agreed to raise, supply, and equip a force for the invasion of Scotland. Such a counter-invasion, they reasoned, would force the Scots to withdraw from Ireland and enable the Confederacy to conquer the rest of the country. The force was to be provided with 2,000 muskets, 24 hundredweight of black powder, match and 200 barrels of oatmeal. Alasdair MacColla was

appointed as leader of the small army. As many as 1,800 troops and followers were shipped to Scotland in early June 1644, although possibly in more than one journey.

The force was divided into three regiments: Lieutenant General Alexander MacDonnell's under the command of Major Thomas Laghtman, Colonel Manus O'Cahan's regiment and that of Colonel James MacDonell's regiment.

The nature of the brigade and its composition can be gleaned from an officer list sent to Ormonde in November 1644. The list names 73 officers, two-thirds with Irish names and the remainder having Lowland Scots, Highland or English (or Anglo-Irish) names in origin. The rank and file were seemingly for the most part recruited from Ulster, and had very likely seen extensive service under Macolla fighting in Ireland. The discipline demonstrated by these units arguably suggests that some officers and men had seen service with the Spanish in Flanders.[1]

The exact arming of these troops is a much-discussed topic. Many have come forward to argue that the absence of pikes in the Confederacy's agreement to supply them as sufficient evidence none or few were carried. However, there is no record of these troops fighting in all musket formations whilst in Ireland. Contemporary writers and accounts of the actions do make reference to the use of pikes, and to the Irish skill with such weapons at such battles as Benburb, in 1646.

This musketeer is very well equipped, having possibly made the most of victories at Tippermuir and Aberdeen and collected new equipment from the spoils left on the field. He is dressed in a pair of white trews, which were considered an easily identifiable mark of 'wilde Irish'. (Painting by Anthony Barton, © Helion & Company Limited)

2. 'Regular' Pikeman.

This soldier is from one of the standing regiments of Highlanders who fought for the Royalist cause during the conflict. A regular, he would have been trained by professional officers, many of whom had seen European service. Wearing a plaid over his shoulder, he could use it as additional adverse weather clothing or as a blanket. His bonnet is based on a brown knitted cap recovered from a bog find at Dava Moor, Cromdale, Morayshire. Other finds on the body date it to no later than 1646. A further brown woollen bonnet was found at Quintfall Hill, Barrock in Caithness. His sword carried on a belt and hanger is another Continental import. (Painting by Anthony Barton, © Helion & Company Limited)

Plate C

'Regular' Cavalry Trooper.

Whilst Montrose could thank his regular infantry for his victories in 1644, those hard-fought battles of 1645 owed much more to the increasing numbers of cavalry that was made available to him. The largest of these cavalry units was the regiment under the leadership of Lord Gordon. Numbering some 400 at its largest, Gordon's regiment was trained and likely equipped as a modern

---

1. See Stephenson, pp.102-107, Reid, *Scots Armies of the 17th Century: The Royalist Armies*, pp.54-58, and Lowe. J, 'The Earl of Antrim and Irish aid to Montrose in 1644', *Irish Sword* IV (1960).

regiment of Harquebusiers. This particular trooper, whilst not equipped with a back and breast plates, is fortunate enough to have been issued a brace of pistols and a quality cavalry sword. Reflecting his country's long association with Sweden, he wears a Swedish 'pot', which like his pistols were imported in great numbers into Scotland during the period. His doublet is hidden beneath a thigh-length riding coat. (Painting by Anthony Barton, © Helion & Company Limited)

Plate D.

Montrose's Irish Brigade at the Battle of Aberdeen, 13 September 1644.

Divisions of pike and musket deploy into firing lines to fight with the centre of the Covenanter Army at Aberdeen.

The principal part of the army was the Irish Brigade made up of three regiments of foot. These units, Laghtnan's, McDonnell's and O'Cahan's may have totalled around some 1,500 men. Following skirmishing on the flanks of his army, Montrose ordered a general advance and following a prolonged firefight in the centre, the Covenanter forces gave way and collapsed into a rout.

The Irish soldiers depicted here are in a mix of Western European and traditional Irish dress, including white trews. Some wear a parochial interpretation of the popular military hat, the Montero. For further notes, see the photo and caption on page 30. (Painting by Peter Dennis, © Helion & Company Limited)

Plate E.

Highlanders.

These are the 'soldiers' of the clan 'regiment'. Whilst not the 'gentlemen' of the clan, who would occupy the front rank of the formation, these clansmen – or rather 'tacksmen' – would occupy a position near to the front. When not fighting they would be working on farms as the tenants of the clan chief and his kinsmen, to whom they would pay rent, or 'tacks' to.

Whilst not attaining the same level of martial proficiency as their betters, they would be expected to acquire and maintain weaponry and equipment commensurate with their status within the clan structure. Not having the discipline and training to work as a modern infantry unit, a clan 'regiment' would probably be able to give a single massed volley in an action, and that would often be prior to the charge to contact.

Three are armed with Dutch muskets, many of which were imported into the British Isles during the Civil Wars. Two are sporting broadswords and the clansman on the far left is carrying a cheap Tuck-style sword.

All four figures illustrate different arrangements for the carrying of powder and ammunition. The first one the left is using bandoliers, whilst the following three use either a powder flask or possibly using pockets or their plaid to carry cartridges in. (Painting by Anthony Barton, © Helion & Company Limited)

Plate F.

1. Irish Pikeman in Scottish dress

After initial successes many of the Irish Brigade would have had the opportunity to be dressed increasingly in the style of their plundered foes. Thus Lowland style 'hodden grey' jackets and breeches as well as Scots blue bonnets may have become increasingly the norm as the initial attire of the Irish Brigade began to wear due to the attrition of campaigning life. A bundle of brown plaid slung over the left shoulder serves as a blanket – the tough latchet shoes or 'brogues' are based on the Dungiven pair from Co Derry. (Photo/Caption: Dave Swift/Interpreter: Hanno Conring © Claíomh 2014)

2. Irish Musketeer.

Despite the experience of the rank and file in the Irish Brigade equipment was allegedly at a premium around the time of early Autumn 1644. This musketeer has but five 'boxes' of powder hanging from his bandolier – and he would be lucky were they all to be filled. Lacking a sword, he carries a 'scian', or a long single edged traditional Gaelic Irish fighting knife from his left hip. His 'cóta mór' woollen coat is based on examples from Leigh (Co Tipperary) and Killery (Co Sligo) and his plain undyed trews are based on a pair from Kilcommon, Co Tipperary. (Photo: Dave Swift/Interpreter: Marcus Byrne © Claíomh 2014)

Bibliography

Primary Sources

Aiazzi. P, *The Embassy in Ireland of Monsignor G.B Rinuccini* (Dublin, 1873)

Baillie, Robert, *Letters and Journals* (Edinburgh, 1842)

Calendar of State Papers Relating to Ireland 1633-1647 (London, 1901)

Calendar of State Papers, Domestic, Charles I 1637-1649 (London, 1897)

Gordon. J, *History of Scots Affairs, 1637-1641* (Aberdeen, 1841)

Gordon, Patrick, of Ruthven, *A short Abridgement of Britaines Distemper 1638-1649* (Aberdeen, 1844)

Morgan, Sir Thomas, 'A true and just relation of Major-General Sir Thomas Morgan's progress…as it was delivered by the General himself', in: *English Civil War Notes and Queries* No.34

Seton, B.G. & J.G. Arnot, *Prisoners of the '45* (Edinburgh, 1928)

Spalding, John, *Memorialls of the Trubles in Scotland 1627-1645* (Aberdeen, 1850)

Vernon, John, *The young Horse-man, or the honest plain-dealing Cavalier*, John Tincey (ed.), (Frome, 1993)

Munro. R, *Monro, his Expedition with the Worthy Scots Regiment (called Mac-Keys Regiment)* (Westport CT, 1999)

Wishart, George, *Memoirs of James, Marquis of Montrose, 1639-1650*, translated by G. Murdoch (London, 1893)

Secondary Sources

Adair, John, *Cheriton 1644* (Kineton, 1973)

Atkin, Malcolm, *Cromwell's Crowning Mercy* (Stroud, 1998)

Barratt, John, *Cavaliers: The Royalist Army at War 1642-46* (Stroud, 2000)

Barthorp, Michael, *Marlborough's Army 1702-11* (London, 1980)

Black, Jeremy, *A Military Revolution? Military Change and European Society 1550-1800* (London, 1991)

Brzezinski, Richard, *The Army of Gustavus Adolphus Volume 2 Cavalry* (London, 1993)

Brzezinski, Richard, *Lützen 1632,* (Oxford, 2001)

Bull, Stephen, *The Furie of the ordnance, Artillery in the English Civil Wars* (Woodbridge, 2008)

Carlton, Charles, *Going to the Wars - The Experience of the British Civil Wars, 1638-1651* (London, 1992)

Chartrand, René, *Louis XIV's Army* (London, 1983)

Childs, John, *Warfare in the Seventeenth Century* (London, 2001)

Davidson, Neil, *The Origins of Scottish Nationhood* (Sterling VA, 2000)

Durham, Keith, *The Border Reivers* (London, 1995)

Dunlevy, Mairead, *Dress in Ireland* (London, 1989)

Edwards, Peter, *Dealing in Death, The Arms Trade and the British Civil Wars, 1638-52* (Stroud, 2000)

Firth, C.H, *Cromwell's Army* (London, 1902)

Furgol, Edward, *A Regimental History of the Covenanting Armies 1639-1651* (Edinburgh, 1990)

Furgol, Edward M., 'Scotland Turned Sweden: The Scottish Covenanters and The Military Revolution, 1638-1651' in *The Scottish National Covenant in its British Context 1638-1651* John Morrill (editor), (Edinburgh, 1990)

Grant, Charles S., *From Pike to Shot 1685-1720* (London, 1986)

Heath, Ian, *Armies of the Sixteenth Century* (Guernsey, 1997)

Heath, Ian, *The Irish Wars 1485-1603* (Oxford, 1993)

Hill, James Michael, *Celtic Warfare 1595-1763* (Edinburgh, 1986)

Hollick, Clive, *The Battle of Benburb 1646* (Cork, 2011)

Hyde, Edward, Earl of Clarendon, *The History of the Great Rebellion,* Roger Lockyer (ed.) (Oxford, 1970)

Leniham, Padraig, 'Celtic' Warfare in the 1640s', in *Celtic Dimensions of the British Civil Wars,* ed. by John R.Young (Edinburgh, 1997)

Lenihan. Padraig, 'The Leinster army and the battle of Dungan's Hill, 1647', in *Irishmen in War, From the Crusades to 1798, Essays from the Irish Sword* Volume 1 (Dublin, 2006)

Loeber, R, & G. Parker, 'The Military Revolution in Seventeenth-century Ireland', in *Ireland from Independence to Occupation 1641-1660,* ed. by J. Ohlmeyer, (Cambridge, 1995)

Macinnes, Allan, *Clanship, Commerce and the House of Stuart 1603-1788* (East Linton, 1996)
Mackenny, Kevin, *The Laggan Army in Ireland 1640-80: The Landed Interests, Political Ideologies and Military Campaigns of the North-West Ulster Settlers'*(Dublin, 2005)
Paterson. Raymond Campbell, *A Land Afflicted, Scotland and the Covenanter Wars 1638-1690* (Edinburgh, 1998)
Parker, Geoffrey, *The Military Revolution, Military Innovation and the rise of the West 1500-1800* (Cambridge, 1988)
Parker, Geoffrey, *The Thirty Years' War* (London, 1984)
Peachey, Stuart, *The Mechanics of Infantry Combat in The First Civil War* (Bristol, 1992)
Reid, Stuart, *Gunpowder Triumphant* (Leigh on Sea, 1987)
Reid, Stuart, *Highland Clansman 1689-1746* (Oxford, 1997)
Reid, Stuart, *The Campaigns of Montrose* (Edinburgh, 1990)
Reid, Stuart. *Scots Armies of the 17th Century - The Royalist Armies 1639-46* (Leigh on Sea, 1989)
Roberts, Michael, 'The Military Revolution 1560-1660', in *The Military Revolution Debate*, Clifford J. Rogers (ed.), (Oxford, 1995)
Silke, John. J, 'The Irish Abroad 1534-1691', in *A New History of Ireland*, Vol. 3. ed. by T.W. Moody, F.J. Bryne & F.X. Martin, (Dublin, 1976)
Stevenson, David, *Highland Warrior: Alasdair MacColla and the Civil Wars* (Edinburgh, 1980)
Tincey, John, *Soldiers of the English Civil War (2): Cavalry* (London, 1990)
Tomasson, C. & F. Buist, *Battles of the '45* (London, 1962)
Wedgwood, C.V, *Montrose* (London, 1952)
Wheeler, James Scott, *Cromwell in Ireland* (Dublin, 1999)
White, Iain, *Agriculture and Society in Seventeenth Century Scotland* (Edinburgh, 1979)
Weigley, Russell, *The Age of Battles* (London, 1991)
Williams, Ronald, *The Heather and the Gale: Clan Donald and Clan Campbell during the Wars of Montrose* (Lochar, 1987)
Williams, Ronald, *Montrose, Cavalier in Mourning* (London, 1975)
Young, Peter, *Marston Moor 1644 - The Campaign and the Battle* (Kineton, 1970)

Articles

Barratt, John, 'A Civil War Artillery Train', in *English Civil War Notes and Queries*, No. 32.
Brzezinski Richard 'British Mercenaries in the Baltic, 1560-1683(2)', in *Military Illustrated* No.6, April/May, 1987.
Casway, Jerrold, 'Unpublished letters of Owen Roe O'Neil', in *Analecta Hibernica*, No.29, 1980
Danachair, Caoimhin O., 'Montrose's Irish Regiments', in *The Irish Sword*, Vol. 4, 1959/60
Duggan. L, 'The Irish Brigade with Montrose', in *Irish Ecclesiastical Review*, 1958
Henshall, Audrey & Wilfred A. Seaby, 'The Dungiven Costume', in *Ulster Journal of Archaeology*Third Series, Vol. 24/25, 1961/1962
Hill, James Michael, 'Killiecrankie and the Evolution of Highland Warfare', in *War in History*, Volume 1, No.2, 1994
Lowe. J, 'The Earl of Antrim and Irish aid to Montrose in 1644', in *The Irish Sword*, Vol. 4 (1960)
Roy, Ian, 'England turned Germany? The Aftermath of The Civil War in its European Context', in *Transactions of the Royal Historical Society*, 5th Series, Volume 28
Williams. Andrew, 'The Ulster Army of the Confederate Catholics 1642-49', in *The Irish Sword*, Vol. 54, Summer 2011

Introducing Claíomh

Claíomh, meaning 'sword' in Irish, is a professional 'living history' group portraying late medieval and early modern military life in Ireland to a museum-quality standard. Composed of like-minded individuals, the group is continually working on a wide range of reconstructive projects.

Of foremost interest to the group are impressions of military personnel of Irish Gaelic lineage c.1480-1660 – from Irish participation in the Battle of Stoke Field in England in 1487 and up to and including the Irish Confederate & Cromwellian Wars fought from the 1640s to the early 1650s.

Claíomh uses only the highest quality re-constructed artefacts available and many of our reproduced weapons are based upon the unique originals kept in the national collections of both jurisdictions – north and south – on the island of Ireland.

Claíomh serves a diverse client-base in various capacities. Events frequently taken on by the membership include corporate events, press releases, private functions, on-site heritage interpretations, parades, clan-rallies, ceremonial guard, in-school/college education and television/film work. Claíomh provides demonstrations as historical/archaeological interpreters and as dramatic stunt-fighters.

They can be contacted at buannacht@gmail.com

Their web site is www.claiomh.ie

The cover artwork of this book is also available as a high quality limited edition print, size 500mm (height) x 700mm (width). Produced in a limited edition of just 500, the first 25 are signed and numbered by the artist, Peter Dennis. To order please visit www.helion.co.uk

Related titles

Cavalier Capital: Oxford in the English Civil War 1642-1646
John Barratt
ISBN 9781910294581 (Hardback)
Early Modern Systems of Command: Queen Anne's Generals, Staff Officers and the Direction of Allied Warfare in the Low Countries and Germany, 1702-1711
Stewart Stansfield
ISBN 9781910294475 (Hardback)
Marlborough's Other Army: The British Army and the Campaigns of the First Peninsula War, 1702-1712
Nick Dorrell
ISBN 9781910294635 (Hardback)